Data-Based Decision Making and Digital Transformation

Data-Based Decision Making and Digital Transformation

Daniel J. Power and Ciara Heavin

 BUSINESS EXPERT PRESS

Data-Based Decision Making and Digital Transformation

First published in 2018 by
Business Expert Press, LLC
222 East 46th Street, New York, NY 10017
www.businessexpertpress.com

ISBN-13: 978-1-63157-658-4 (paperback)
ISBN-13: 978-1-63157-659-1 (e-book)

Business Expert Press Information Systems Collection

Collection ISSN: 2156-6577 (print)
Collection ISSN: 2156-6593 (electronic)

Cover and interior design by Exeter Premedia Services Private Ltd., Chennai, India

First edition: 2018

10 9 8 7 6 5 4 3 2 1

Printed in the United States of America.

Abstract

Many organizations must adapt to survive digital disruption. One approach is digital transformation. The quest for transformation is a journey and the destination is not fixed. Rather senior managers must envision a data-centric organization and encourage data-based decision-making processes.

Data-based decision making is an ongoing process of collecting and analyzing different types of data from diverse sources. Building better decision support and using analytics is an enabler of more effective decision making and digital transformation. Digital transformation changes people's behavior, organizational processes, and technologies to enhance performance and better meet customer needs. Using data becomes part of an organization's culture and managers learn to use data and analytics appropriately for each decision situation. Analytics and decision support become pervasive and enhance data-based decision making.

Digital disruption is like a tidal wave. Managers must learn to act quickly using data. To succeed in the long-run, managers must ensure that data is used ethically. Both data visualization and data story telling can assist managers in directing the digital journey. Algorithms, Artificial Intelligence, and Machine Learning are tools to make processes faster and smarter.

Middle managers using data-based decision-making are the key to successfully implementing a digital vision.

Keywords

analytics, artificial intelligence, big data, business intelligence, competitive advantage, data, data storytelling, data-based decision making, decision making, decision support, decision support systems, digital transformation, IoT, machine learning, managers, visualization

pervasive   approach   timely

analytics   telling   technologies Machine

           outcomes   effective

data-based   roles improve   situation   ethically

    interpreting   unique

make   processes   making   iterative   disruption

                      Development

customer necessary   more   digital

executing Both strategy successful adapt

deliver

become   decision   survive   process

data-centric   need

support   transformation   Artifical

directing used faster ongoing   better

        analyzing streamlined   organization

    Many especially Middle   assess journey

importance   accurate   data

maturity   decisions   analyses

    culture

important   managers

Abstract of Power, D. and C. Heavin, Data-based Decision Making and Digital Transformation, 2018

Contents

Preface

For many years, both of us have been working with digital technologies and computerized decision support and analytics. Over the years, we have observed both successes and failures, shattered expectations for new decision support systems, ongoing technology obsolescence, and magnificent technology innovations. We have experienced digital transformation in many industries, including retailing at Amazon, streaming video at Netflix, transportation at Uber, and accommodations at Airbnb. Computing and information technologies have changed the world and will continue to do so.

This book is wide ranging in its coverage of digital transformation, but it is primarily focused upon how expanding data sources can improve data-based decision making and help realize successful changes in organizations. The goal of the book is to help managers anticipate and thrive in the disruptive, data intensive digital environment facing many organizations.

Writing this book has been a transformative journey for us and we acknowledge it builds on the prior ideas of many researchers, experts, and bloggers. For more than a year, we have explored the riddle of how managers can cope with digital disruption. We found consensus that the competitive problem of digitalization was real. We found examples of entrepreneurs and managers implementing new business models and taking strategic actions intended to use digital technologies for competitive advantage. In some cases, actions seemed short term and mere repairs to outdated processes, rather than significant changes to processes and business models. In other cases, the transformation was innovative and extraordinarily successful.

This book is targeted for managers, especially middle-level managers who are trying to come to grips with using data-based decision making in a transforming organization. We encourage managers to practice thoughtful, ethical, data-based decision making.

Acknowledgments

Many people over the years have contributed to the ideas and advice developed in this book—our students, readers of Decision Support News, faculty colleagues, friends in various software companies, and friends associated with the BeyeNETWORK, a TechTarget company. Also, DSS-Resources.com and Decision Support News have been effective ways to communicate ideas and to get feedback.

Actual production of this book is the result of the efforts of many people. Thanks to everyone at Business Expert Press (BEP) and affiliated organizations.

Lastly, and most importantly, we want to acknowledge the invaluable help and support of our families. Dan thanks his wife Carol and sons Alex, Ben, and Greg. Ciara sends thanks to her husband Finian, sons Oisin and Ronan, and to her Mum and Dad.

Our families motivated us to make this contribution toward improving data-based decision making in organizations and helping managers and their organizations survive well in a disrupted, digital world.

CHAPTER 1

Introduction and Overview

The year 1951 marks the beginning of the first wave of economic and social digital disruption and transformation. The first commercially available digital computer was the Ferranti Mark I, an English digital computer released in February 1951. A much more famous and commercially successful digital computer, the Universal Automatic Computer (UNIVAC) was released in March 1951.

The vacuum tube computers of 1951 have become solid state, miniaturized devices. Digital computers and specialized software replaced many thousands of bookkeepers and their ledger books. The Sears, Roebuck, and Montgomery Ward merchandise catalogs are defunct, replaced by online shopping at sites like Amazon.com. Rotary dial phones were replaced by various digital technologies over the years; communication is now dominated by the ubiquitous smart phone. Black and White over the air television displayed using cathode ray tubes (CRT) has been replaced by streaming media provided over the Internet on digital displays. Hand-written, personal letters have been largely replaced by E-mail and social media. These, and many other large-scale changes, have resulted from the initial waves of digital transformation. We have seen incredible data-enabled changes. Digital disruption is continuing, and the possibilities for change have expanded.

Many organizations must change to survive digital disruption, and managers in those organizations must create and pursue what can be called a digital transformation strategy. Some sources estimate that 90 percent of all the data in the world today has been created in the last few years. According to a number of estimates, 2.5 exabytes, equivalent to 2.5 quintillion bytes,[1] of data are generated every day. Research group IDC

---

[1] http://iflscience.com/technology/how-much-data-does-the-world-generate-every-minute/

estimates that 163 zettabytes of data will be created each year by 2025.[2] Global society is in the midst of a profound and irreversible change. Data are everywhere, we are dependent on digital devices, and data provide an opportunity for innovative business models, increased efficiencies, and greater effectiveness in meeting customer needs.

Managers must at a fundamental level make better use of data and facts in decision making. Facts should guide digital transformation and digital transformation initiatives should increase the use of data and facts in every activity and process of an organization including decision making. Analyzing data is now a core decision support task in many businesses as managers try to derive value from the large volume of diverse data sources. Digitization of business activities and processes has led to an explosive growth in data. The "Big Data" tsunami has hence increased the need for business and data analytics. This major change has heightened the need for managers to understand the possibilities of these technologies and their application in a variety of areas including consumer financial services, insurance, manufacturing, media, retail, pharmaceuticals, health care, and government.[3]

As senior managers formulate information technology (IT) strategies, formulate a digital transformation vision, and assess investments, it is essential to use data-based decision making and data analytics to investigate and evaluate choices. Managers should ask if the investments will improve organizational decision making, knowledge management, yield valued digital transformation, and ultimately enhance organizational success? According to Grossman (2016), "Organizations that foster a culture of making data-based decisions will be in a stronger position to weather the changes ahead." We agree.

Digital transformation strategy involves making decisions about technology trade-offs and ideally choices are data-informed and fact-based. Data-based decision making is both a process and a culture. Some

[2] IDC, Data Age at https://seagate.com/files/www-content/our-story/trends/files/Seagate-WP-DataAge2025-March-2017.pdf

[3] Grossman, R. 2016. "The Industries that are Being Disrupted the Most by Digital." *Harvard Business Review*. https://hbr.org/2016/03/the-industries-that-are-being-disrupted-the-most-by-digital. March 21, 2016.

managers and organizations already value using data and facts to make decisions. Part of successful digital transformation is making systematic use of data in decision making. Data-based decision making, using data and facts to make decisions, is both a prerequisite to digital transformation and the result of a data-informed culture. Improved data-based decision making is and should be a necessary consequence of a digital transformation vision and strategy.

Global business activity is accelerating and decision-making activities and processes must be responsive to changing business needs and a high velocity decision environment. Understanding what is occurring can increase the adaptive response of managers. Awareness is a major goal of the following chapters. In general, it is not sufficient to only understand the need for new technology-supported processes, for better use of data in decision making and the possibilities for revised and innovative business models to achieve positive change. Managers must understand how to successfully implement digital transformation competitive opportunities. Managers must think digital and be committed to building data capture and data use into core activities and processes. A transformation strategy without an implementation plan and action taking is wishful thinking.

Improved data-based decision making skills of middle-level managers and use of analytical tools and innovative computerized decision support can reduce the negative consequences and chaos some organizations are experiencing due to digital technologies and vast, ever-increasing, amounts of data. Data-based decision making can help channel information technology changes in positive directions that are essential to successful digital transformation and improved organization viability. Relying solely on programmed data-driven decision making using algorithms and reducing the number of decision makers in an organization is only a partial solution for digital transformation and then only in some industries. Replacing decision makers with decision automation, programmed data-driven decision making, and decision management has a serious downside for society and may actually increase digital disruption and make positive digital transformation in an organization less likely.

To cope with digital disruption, many managers should learn new knowledge and new skills, including the basics of analytics, data-based decision making, and digital transformation technologies. This short book is a starting point, a primer. The following chapters discuss decision making and digital transformation, data-based decision making, high velocity decision making and analytics, and implementing digital transformation. These chapters help managers become data-based decision makers who can assess, choose, and successfully implement digital transformation competitive opportunities. The remaining chapters emphasize the how and what questions of data-based decision making and digital transformation.

Each of the following chapters serves as a guide to help managers actively confront the challenge of implementing and using data-based decision making in a digitally transforming global business ecosystem. Our objectives are both ambitious and modest. We explore a number of broad questions: (1) How can managers become data-based decision makers? (2) How can digital transformation become part of an organizational strategy? (3) What new skills do managers need to implement digital transformation? and (4) How will we know an organization has been successfully transformed?

CHAPTER 2

Decision Making and Digital Transformation

Digital transformation is changing our lives, our jobs, our organizations, and our world. Each of us makes choices that impact how we use digital data and digital technology. Managers and organizations that do not keep up with digital transformation trends and successfully implement key transformation projects will likely suffer negative consequences, including loss of jobs, going out of business, or being acquired by a digital upstart or a more traditional competitor.[1]

Innovating with data, digital technologies, and data-based decision making is a major business opportunity that can change business models, improve customer experiences, reduce costs and increase agility. Such innovation is necessary to prosper in our changing global economic markets. Sadly, there is no simple formula or training program that can help managers become data-based decision makers. Indeed, most managers are trying to learn "on the job" to understand what digital transformation means for them, their team, and their organization while trying to tackle the great challenge presented by rapidly expanding organizational data. Successful digital organizational transformation requires that managers have mastered data-based decision-making skills that can help formulate, implement and manage an appropriate digital transformation strategy.

Effective data-based decision making using accurate and timely data is integral to successful digital transformation. Opportunities and obstacles created by digitalization[2] and leveraging digital technologies require that

---

[1] "Couchbase Research Reveals a Majority of Organizations Expect to Fail in Four Years if Digital Transformation Approach is Unsuccessful." http://dssre-sources.com/news/4798.php

[2] https://i-scoop.eu/digitization-digitalization-digital-transformation-disruption/

managers develop sophisticated data analysis, data interpretation, and decision-making skills. The velocity at which large datasets are processed and reported requires that managers adapt to an increasingly fast paced business environment. A digital world requires decision making and leadership skills that leverage diverse data sources, data analytics know-what and know-how, and decision support capabilities that enable and support the strategic direction of an organization.

Data-based decision making is not a new idea. Decision support research began at the dawn of the digital age and the concepts of decision support and decision support systems (DSS) remain understandable and intuitively descriptive. Related terms such as high velocity decision making, data analytics, business intelligence, and big data analytics are of more recent origin and are interpreted in different ways by managers, software vendors, and consultants. Also, artificial intelligence (AI), data-based applications, and real-time analytics are accelerating the velocity of digital organizational transformation.[3]

Data-based decision making is a broad concept that prescribes an ongoing process of collecting and analyzing different types of data to aid in making fact-based, routine and nonroutine decisions. The use of new digital information technologies is generating more data to change and improve business processes, alter business models, enhance products, and change customer experiences.

Many new technology developments, like the Internet of Things (IoT) are expanding the range of computing devices and expanding data collection. AI and data analytics are helping managers use the new data sources in real-time. Managers choose how to exploit and adopt these technology developments. Actions of managers disrupt existing business models and create new opportunities for businesses across industry sectors. These intertwined changes are causing significant digital disruptions.

The following five sections in this chapter discuss related topics, including: (1) data, information, and knowledge, paying particular attention to the opportunities to use new data sources as part of a digital transformation strategy, (2) understanding data-based decisions and decision

---

[3] Dimension Data, "Artificial Intelligence and Analytics Accelerate the Pace of Digital Workplace Transformation." http://dssresources.com/news/4789.php

support, (3) digital transformation impacts, especially upon people, processes, and strategy, (4) asking the right questions, and (5) creating data-centric organizations. Our perspective emphasizes the centrality of decision support and data-based decision making in organizations.

Understanding Data, Information, and Knowledge

To adapt and cope, organization decision makers need better, faster, more accurate data and information to make decisions. The volume, availability, and speed of real-time data continue to be a special challenge in organizations. Managers are increasingly focused on finding opportunities arising from valuable data insights. An organization's capability to capture, store and manage, analyze and visualize large volumes of semistructured, and unstructured data is generally referred to as using "Big Data" (Chen et al. 2012). Big data refers to very large data volumes that are complex and varied, and often collected and must be analyzed in real-time. Venture Capitalist Bryce Roberts[4] reminds us "Data, big, medium or small, has no value in and of itself. The value of data is unlocked through context and presentation." How data are presented or visualized can change behavior. Managers continue to struggle with issues like managing large volumes of data and information, anticipating external environmental uncertainty, and monitoring advances in technology.

Focusing on greater use of knowledge as an organizational strategy found widespread recognition and approval after Drucker (1992) concluded that "the basic economic resource—the means of production—is no longer capital, nor natural resources, nor labor. It is and will be knowledge." While knowledge remains a core organizational and societal resource, the notion of big data and developing and understanding an organization's ability to extract relevant knowledge and associated insights using sophisticated technology has of necessity become a priority for managers.

A vast amount of industry, company, product, and customer data can be gathered from a wide variety of external and Internet sources including online social media forums, web blogs, social networking sites, logs of website visits, and retail transactions. Most of this data is significant in

---

[4] Roberts, B. February 2012. "Data Data Everywhere and Not a Drop of Value," http://bryce.vc blog, at URL http://bryce.vc/post/15300645787/data-data-everywhere-and-not-a-drop-of-value

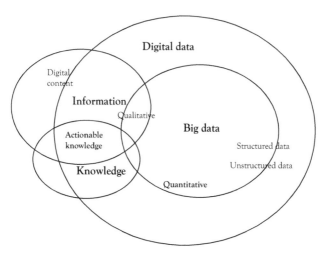

Figure 2.1 Data concept map: Big data, data, information, and knowledge

volume and it is often unstructured in nature—it is considered big data. It is difficult to prescribe a "one size fits all" approach to big data because big data for one organization may be "small data" for another. However, the key to successful big data use is a manager's ability to identify the value in the data collected and devise ways to explore and extract value from large volumes of data for the right people at the right time.

There is overlap and yet differences among the concepts of digital data, information, knowledge, and big data (see Figure 2.1). It is difficult to identify where one concept begins and another ends, this challenge is reflected in the distinct lack of a common language used by stakeholders when it comes to defining and discussing these phenomena. Rather than over emphasizing the boundaries of data, knowledge, and information and when data becomes big data, managers must focus on decision support and analytics needs required to help them in achieving business objectives. Managers need relevant data, information, knowledge and decision support capabilities to meet decision making needs.

Understanding Decisions and Decision Support

Managers make many decisions and the characteristics of each decision determine if analytics and decision support are appropriate and if so what support is most useful. Decisions are made as part of processes and decisions result in outcomes. A decision may involve assessing and evaluating alternatives using data sets, variables, and algorithms. The quality of a decision is often impacted by the type of process or path that is pursued in making and implementing a decision. Organizational decision environments are typically characterized by a rational decision making approach. Rationality is the quality of being consistent with or based on logic and reason. One hopes managers and responsible decision makers attempt to be rational and thoughtful in their decision making.

Decisions vary widely in structure and complexity. Some decisions are characterized by a concise decision question, with a clear, well defined and structured choice. These are typically known as operating or function-specific decisions. This type of decision is usually routine, occurring regularly and frequently, that is, daily or weekly. Tactical decisions are typically addressing a broader decision question, and are semistructured in nature, this means that some but not all of the information necessary to make the decision is available. These decisions are mostly internally focused and may even be specific to an individual business unit. Other nonroutine decisions are more complex. In these situations, some variables may not be well understood, often information required to make the decision is unavailable, incomplete and in some situations information may be known to be inaccurate. Classified as strategic decisions, these are usually complex, unstructured decisions involving many different and connected parts. These decisions usually involve a high degree of uncertainty about outcomes. If implemented, strategic decisions often result in major changes in an organization. Pursuing digital transformation is a strategic decision.

Modern decision support is evolving rapidly in step with computing hardware and software progress. A modern decision support system is up-to-date technologically. The modern era in decision support development started in many ways in 1995 with the specification of HTML 2.0 and the introduction of handheld computing and cell phones. Since 2007, Web 2.0 technologies, mobile integrated devices, and improved software development tools have revolutionized decision support user interfaces, while the decision support data store back-end has gotten extremely powerful supporting large, real-time and complex data sets. Modern decision support is varied and increasingly widespread in use.

A DSS is a computer-based information system that supports individual or team decision making. There are five major categories or types of DSS, but some DSS do not fit neatly into one of the categories, instead they have multiple decision support functionalities and a hybrid architecture. Hybrid or complex DSS have components to provide more than one category of decision support. The five primary DSS categories include: (1) Communication-driven DSS that enable cooperation, supporting more than one person working on a shared task, (2) Data-driven DSS that emphasize access to and manipulation of internal company data integrated with external data, (3) Document-driven DSS that manage, retrieve, and manipulate semistructured or well-structured documents, (4) Knowledge-driven DSS that provide specialized problem-solving expertise stored as rules, procedures, or in similar structures, and (5) Model-driven DSS that emphasize access to and manipulation of statistical, financial, optimization, simulation, or other quantitative models.

The general, defining characteristics of DSS have not changed over the years. These systems remain characterized by facilitation, interaction, an ancillary role, repeated use, task oriented, identifiable and having a decision impact (cf. Power 2002). Some characteristics are more closely associated with one category of DSS than another, but complex DSS often have multiple subsystems that fit in different categories. For example, a complex, modern decision support capability may have a well-defined data-driven subsystem and a model-driven subsystem. Major specific characteristics of modern DSS include: (1) Broad domain of applications with diverse functionality, (2) Faster access to data stored in very large data sets, (3) Faster deployment, (4) Faster response, (5) Integrated DSS with transaction processing systems (TPS), (6) Lower cost per user, (7) Multiuser and collaborative interaction, (8) Real-time data and real-time DSS use, (9) Ubiquitous, (10) User friendly and a better user experience, and (11) Visualization. Table 2.1 describes these 11 characteristics of modern decision support capabilities. These modern decision support applications enhance both data-based and data-informed decision making.

This list of attributes and characteristics of a modern DSS is likely incomplete. Decision support is usually ahead of current practices, but the list may represent current "best practices." Those of us interested in modern computerized decision support are promoting new ideas and

Table 2.1 Characteristics of modern decision support applications

Characteristic	Description
1. Broad domain of applications with diverse functionality	Decision support user base and the rationale for DSS use has expanded. There are many use cases for decision support and we are capturing use case models.
2. Faster access to data stored in very large data sets	Data access refers to software and activities related to retrieving or acting upon data in a database or other repository. Data-driven DSS can use very large data stores.
3. Faster deployment	Software deployment is all of the activities that make a new DSS available for use. Faster deployment is partly due to the use of Web technologies, also better prototyping and templates.
4. Faster response	How quickly an interactive system responds to user input has improved significantly. In a distributed computing environment, the lag for video, voice, data retrieval or transmitting results is now negligible.
5. Integrated DSS with TPS	Enterprisewide decision support applications are increasingly common. A standardized interface and single sign-on security helps create an integrated and unified decision support/transaction processing environment (TPS).
6. Lower cost per user	Total annual cost for licensing development software on a per user basis is declining. This trend will continue given the increased open source decision support applications.
7. Multiuser and collaborative interaction	DSS are increasingly collaborative with shared decision making environments.
8. Real-time data and real-time DSS use	The classical decision support idea is an immediate real-time system that is used while action is occurring. That vision is increasingly possible and useful.
9. Ubiquitous	DSS are available and seem to be usable everywhere. DSS for a particular function can be used on mobile devices.
10. User friendly and a better user experience	Usability is the ease of using a particular tool. All DSS are much easier to use, but we can do more to improve usability and reduce information load.
11. Visualization	Creating images, diagrams, or animations to communicate a message is important. Modern DSS include capabilities to create and manipulate visualizations.

approaches, and encouraging progress in supporting decision making. Building better decision support provides one of the "keys" to competing in this increasingly digital global business environment. Better decision support is a major enabler of digital transformation.

Digital Transformation Impacts

Digital transformation is a complex concept and challenging goal that holds a variety of meanings for a diverse set of stakeholders. In a recent Forbes article, Kerschberg (2017) contends that technology is central to organizational digital transformation, in particular adopting analytics, big data, mobile, cloud, IoT, and application development. While technology may be at the core of digital transformation, successful digital transformation requires excellent leadership, a supportive culture, and new business processes. Leadership should promote and cultivate a data-based decision-making culture. Digital transformation remains a complex task. It begins with strategic leadership and a commitment to a digital transformation organization strategy.

Barriers to entry for many industries have been lowered and some industries have been consolidated or forced to contract. Nontraditional competitors are entering industries and changing markets and goods and services. Few managers in traditional industries led prior transformations and some have been caught off-guard. Managers should have known digital technologies would be an enabler of change, so why were so many surprised by the suddenness and magnitude of the disruption? Lack of vision and understanding? Complacency? An inward looking attitude? Lack of knowledge? Perhaps a combination of these reasons.

A related discussion on digital transformation, cf. Power (2017), stated that a strategic vision for digital transformation is useful; however vision must be grounded in customer needs and technology possibilities. Indeed, business transformation cannot happen without people making decisions about technology. Figure 2.2 is a conceptual decision support guide for managers.

The conceptual model in Figure 2.2 highlights three levels of organizational tasks for implementing digital transformation including: (1) strategic tasks, (2) tactical tasks, and (3) operational tasks. Managers at each level choose from a set of tasks that should be completed as part of an organization's approach to digital transformation. Through the completion of some or all of these tasks, organizations can move from an ad-hoc approach to a more systematic, mature approach to digital

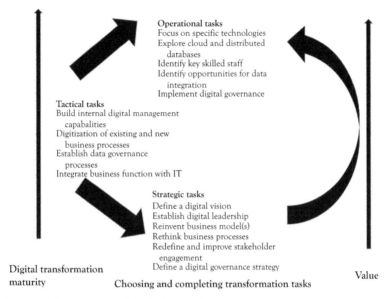

Figure 2.2 Conceptual digital transformation support guide

transformation. Achieving a digital transformation vision that is stable and "mature" comes from successfully completing transformation tasks.

Digital transformation tasks may be broadly characterized in terms of changing people, processes, and technology. For any business strategy to be successful activities across these dimensions need to be aligned. In a Harvard Business Review article, Trevor and Varcoe (2017) promote the notion of strategies, capabilities, and resources to achieve digital transformation including systems that "should be arranged to support the enterprise's purpose." Identifying appropriate transformation tasks to undertake is important.

Strategic tasks represent a high level collection of activities that implement a digital transformation vision and strategy. Some of these tasks include developing the vision, developing digital leadership capability (Westerman et al. 2014), reinventing business models, rethinking business processes, redefining stakeholder engagement (Kerschberg 2017), and developing a digital governance strategy (Ernst and Young 2017). While this list is not exhaustive, it is moving toward a more balanced and holistic approach for managers to tackle digital transformation of an organization.

As illustrated by the "middle out" notation and arrows used in Figure 2.2, tactical tasks (the middle) are integral to the success of a digital transformation strategy. Trevor and Varcoe (2017) refer to this mediating managerial level in terms of building organizational capabilities. At this level, it is important for managers to consider and select tasks that provide them with the means (capability) to deliver the digital transformation strategy. These tactical tasks will drive the digital transformation agenda in an organization with managers asking questions about how transformation can be achieved based on the capabilities available. Tactical tasks are concerned with designing new business processes, establishing disruptive new business models, and defining data governance processes. It is also useful to consider new mechanisms for evaluating performance in terms of achieving digital transformation. Completing tactical tasks may be an opportunity for managers to define new measures of organizational success including understanding customer engagement and customer experience. Data-based decision making should guide and help prioritize tasks.

Operational tasks are focused around the questions managers need to answer for (1) selecting and developing technologies, (2) establishing viable data integration platforms, (3) choosing necessary security controls that will balance data access with data protection, and (4) identifying and developing the right people capabilities to achieve the digital vision for the organization. Managers need to select and complete tasks that develop "assets that will be useful in a digitally transformed world" (cf. Capgemini Consulting 2011).

Completing the appropriate mix of tasks should increase the chances of a successful digital transformation. Technological maturity is at the heart of achieving real digital transformation. To begin a digital transformation journey, managers need to move beyond focusing on new individual technologies to develop a comprehensive digital technology capability that is closely aligned to a well-defined digital transformation vision and strategy.

Digital transformation can both solve problems and create new problems. Successful digital transformation creates a positive, long-term, net benefit for an organization. Applying digital technologies can create a data-based virtuous feedback cycle that leads to adopting and choosing more innovative and transformative digital solutions.

Finding Success: Asking the Right Questions

Making decisions often involves answering questions like "What should be done?" or "What alternative is best?" Asking the right questions can help people make better decisions. Kipling (1902) wrote a poem managers should remember when thinking about defining decision questions. The poem begins "I keep six honest serving-men (They taught me all I knew); Their names are What and Why and When and How and Where and Who." These six are the primary question words. There are other question words and phrases like How many? and How much?, even the word "Is" can start a question, but Kipling's six words (see Figure 2.3) are a good starting place for examining how decision questions differ in intent and how they are similar.

A decision question asks about what action(s) to take among various options or alternatives. A decision process helps create alternatives/options, find them, and sometimes eliminate options. Answering or resolving a decision question should be a thoughtful and comprehensive process. Assessing and understanding the decision question provides guidance and direction for customizing an appropriate decision process. So let's examine Kipling's "serving men" and evaluate what they mean for decision making processes.

What ... ? is a complex word to begin a question. A "**What**" question may seek an approximation, a forecast or an estimate, that is, "What will sales be in the next quarter?" Alternatively a "**What**" question may seek specific facts or information, that is, "What is the current profitability of XYZ?" In this second case, the "**What**" question does not or should not require a decision, rather a fact is sought.

Figure 2.3 Six honest serving men (adapted from Kipling)

Why ... ? questions are the most perplexing and most troublesome. By asking why, a person is expecting a reason for an action or event or an explanation of something that has occurred. Asking and answering why questions are important in problem solving. Understanding causes and motivations helps us understand a decision situation. In general, a "why" question supports reasoning or informs a decision question. For example, examine this question, "Why did sales decline in the last quarter?" This diagnostic question seeks to know the cause of a problem so that perhaps a decision can be made about how to remove the cause and reduce the negative consequences. A person may ask multiple "Why" questions in a decision situation prior to or after asking a key decision question, that is, "How can the decline in sales be stopped or reversed?"

When ... ? refers to time. One wants information about the time or timing of events or actions. The Cambridge English Dictionary notes "We can use when to ask for information about what time something happens." So a decision maker may want to know about past, present or future time, that is, "When did sales start to decline?" "When should the new sales and marketing plan be implemented?" Some **When** questions imply a decision is needed while others are informational. Helper words like will and should can indicate whether information or a decision is sought.

How ... ? much or how many or how can. How is sometimes the indicator of a decision question. For example, similar to the prior discussion we might ask "How can we stop the sales decline?" or "How many people will attend the event?" or "How do we contact customers?" Some how questions are requesting an estimate or conclusion. For example, "How much will a new production facility cost?" Many questions that begin with the how keyword request information rather than a decision, that is, "How do I find XXX?"

Where ... ? refers to location and place. The where question word seems to be primarily an indicator of a need for information about location, that is, "Where will the event be held?" or "Where is the salesperson?" The first location question may involve a decision if phrased with the should helper word, that is, "Where **should** the event be held?"

Finally, there comes **Who ... ?** the who keyword may indicate a request for information or a need to make a decision. For example, "Who is the sales manager?" is an information request. While the question "Who should be the sales manager?" implies the need for a decision among a set of people who have applied for a job. A **Who** question may refer to choosing one person or a group or team of people. Consider the question "Who will implement the new strategy?" The answer might be a single individual or a group or team.

Some decision questions are highly structured, routine and repetitive, others are semistructured or unstructured and even novel and nonroutine. The amount of structure depends to some extent upon the decision situation. For example, for a salesperson the following are usually routine and repetitive questions: "Who will buy the product or service from you and your company?" "What and how much will they buy from you?" "Why do they need the product or service?" and "How should you engage them in a meaningful conversation about the product/service?" In the context of assessing the introduction of a new product, the same questions are more unstructured and often nonroutine.

Although decision questions often begin with one of the six questions words, that is, what, why, when, how, where, and who, these question words get altered by helper words like will and should, much and many. In English, one finds decision questions are alternatively framed as "Should we" or "Should I do XX or go to XX." Colloquial or informal language also interferes with recognizing decision questions. Knowing what the word phrase implies helps us provide decision support when that is appropriate. Asking the "right" decision questions in a solution oriented manner is an important skill for data-based decision makers. Spend some time early in a decision process to specify an appropriate decision question or questions that can be answered.

Creating a Data-Centric Organization

A supportive organizational culture is important to successful digital transformation. A data-centric organization has policies and a culture that encourage and reward the use of data in products, processes, and decision making. Using data to make decisions in organizations has long been a goal of most managers. Using "gut instincts" and limited facts has serious risks. Basing a decision on self-interest is poor practice, and even if that is the choice criterion the decision maker still requires facts. Consulting mystics/fortune-tellers fell into disfavor long ago. Today most decision makers have increased access to more and better data in near real time almost anywhere in the world. This new reality has changed the decision support possibilities. Managers can make better fact-based decisions if they choose to develop the decision support capabilities and infrastructure.

Becoming a data-informed, or data-centric organization has become a priority for many managers. Analytics and decision support must be aligned with business strategy to realize benefits from digital transformation. Pushing for more data and more analytics without a strategic fit is folly. Organizations and managers need to understand what they are trying to achieve. Decision support initiatives fail when there is poor alignment with the business strategy.

Organizations can empower employees with access to relevant data and analytics. The key is to provide relevant data when it is needed to make a decision. The decision maker remains central to decision taking, but technology and analytics support are enhanced for data-based decision making. Providing data does not mean however it will be used properly or even used. Training and reward systems are key to making the new decision support capabilities a factor in improving organizational performance.

The term digital data refers to facts, figures, and digital content captured in information systems. Raw data are the bits and bytes stored electronically. Data may be streaming to a decision maker or retrieved from a static data store. Figuring out what data is relevant and what that data means in a decision situation can be challenging. Data can overwhelm a decision maker and can mislead. Data-based decision making requires anticipating data and analysis needs and providing the opportunity to request and analyze additional data. Analytics involves processes for identifying and communicating patterns, derived conclusions and facts. Decision support and analytics must provide timely and useful information for benefits of digital transformation to be realized.

Using data in decision making **must** become part of an organization's culture. The quest for understanding, formalizing, and prioritizing important decision questions, and then capturing and making available appropriate data, and relevant analysis **must** become an urgent requirement and ongoing priority. A data-centric organization survives and hopefully prospers based on the quality, provision, and availability of data to decision-makers. Data should be captured where it is generated and then it must be appropriately stored and managed for use in decision-making. Analytics, decision support, and data become the basis for decision making in a digitally transformed organization.

Summary

Creating a data-centric organization where managers make data-based decisions has both technology and human resource challenges. Technology challenges continue to evolve as more data and better, easier to use analytic tools become available. The human resource challenge involves retraining and motivating current employees to use analytics, model-driven, and data-driven decision support.

Digital transformation does not occur quickly, rather it is a journey. We know that factors other than data availability influence choices. Without data and facts, then luck and chance dominate outcomes in situations. Chapter 3 examines how using data and information underpin data-based decision making which is also the key to more effective decision making.

CHAPTER 3

Data-Based Decision Making

Some managers seem preoccupied with making better use of current data—internal operations data, customer/client/patient data, supplier data, and market data to name a few data sources. Major data challenges are many including the increasing volumes of varied data, mixed data quality, data security, changing data regulations, generating insights from data, using analytics better, and identifying new opportunities to derive value from data. At the heart of implementing a successful digital transformation strategy is solving two key challenges: (1) managers must understand the value of current data and existing data sources, and (2) managers must have appropriate technology tools, skills, and techniques to support the digital vision. Successful transformation is about more than using current data.

Now let's begin to tackle these challenges to effective data-based decision making and implementing a digital transformation strategy. The following five sections of this chapter discuss: (1) different approaches to managerial decision making including data-based, data-driven, and data-informed, (2) the need for computerized decision support, (3) key skills required for data-based decision making, (4) steps for making data-based decisions, and (5) the importance of data-based decision making for gaining an organizational competitive advantage. To overcome data challenges, one must determine how data can be used to help improve managerial and organizational decision making processes and hence business outcomes. Some people advocate for data-driven decision making, others for data-based or data-informed decision making. The next section explores these differing approaches to using data in decision making.

Data-Based, Data-Driven, and Data-Informed Decision Making

Decision makers are confronted with evolving and expanding data resources and there is a pressing need to ask better questions to help solve real business problems. One can read a variety of case studies about how using data can improve decisions in many domains including education, retail sales, health care, and financial services. Using more data and analytics is often identified as the key to success in these situations.

A number of phrases have been used by authors and consultants to describe the increasing use of data to improve decision making in organizations. The word data is modified as data-based, data-driven, or sometimes data-informed decision making. These phrases are often used interchangeably to refer to an improved organizational decision support capability. While the terms are related, there are important differences. After reviewing prior usage, we find it most useful to focus on data-based decision making. We consider each of these concepts as mutually exclusive, but in some situations complementary. For managers to meaningfully engage with data opportunities and challenges they need to understand how these decision making approaches can be formulated, managed and exploited as part of an organizational digital transformation strategy. Let's examine these three approaches to using data in decision making.

Data-based decision making refers to an ongoing process of collecting and analyzing different types of data to aid in decision making (Power 2017). Decisions are based on data facts, values and vision, intuition, and ethical guidelines. Data-based decision making usually incorporates many diverse data types from a variety of sources including quantitative data balanced with "softer" data that is more descriptive in nature. Data-based decisions are primarily based on data, but analysis and judgment are also very important. Ethical decision making should be incorporated in data-based decision making. Decision makers should apply moral rules, codes, or principles to guide choices for right and truthful behavior.

Data-driven decision making or data-driven management is widely used in articles, consultant reports, white papers and more recently in academic research papers to characterize a particular type of decision making. Data-driven decision making refers to the collection and analysis of data to make decisions, but the data determines the action. Data "drive" the decision making and decisions are made using verifiable data. Some consider data-driven as synonymous with business intelligence, while other authors link the phrase to decision automation. Provost and Fawcett (2013) define data-driven decision making very broadly as "the practice of basing decisions on the analysis of data rather than purely on intuition." According to a number of sources (McAfee and Brynjolfsson 2012; Frick 2014), organizations that use "data-driven decision making" are more productive and more profitable than their competitors. In these research studies respondents likely had various understanding of data-driven decision making.

Data-driven, data-informed or fact-based decision making means managers use and evaluate data to make decisions, but providing more data is not necessarily the way to improve decision making effectiveness. As a concept, data-driven decision making is often used in conjunction with big data and data analytics, particularly quantitative/statistical analytics.

Data-informed decision making is a term used when data and facts are an influential factor in decision making, but not the only factor. According to Maycotte (2015), decisions are complex phenomena that require significant human input in terms of experience and instinct. Maycotte believes, he believes that decisions should not be purely "driven" by data but data may be used to support experienced decision makers to be faster and more flexible in their decision making. He advocates that decision makers need to "strike the balance between expertise and understanding information." The U.S. Department of Education prefers the terms data-based or data-informed decision making over data-driven decision making asserting that decisions should not be based solely on quantitative data.

Using data in decision making should be contingent on the decision situation. Figure 3.1 suggests a continuum of decision situations ranging from highly structured and routine to highly unstructured and nonroutine and recommends different decision making depending on the situation.

Data-driven decision making can be used effectively in highly structured situations when appropriate data and analytics are available. As a

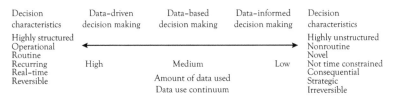

Figure 3.1 Using data in decision making

decision situation becomes more unstructured, the best one can do is data-based decision making because more qualitative content and subjective assessment is needed. It is appropriate and recommended to base a decision upon quantitative and qualitative data in these semistructured decision situations, but other factors like data quality, data relevance, and data timeliness must be resolved. Finally, in highly unstructured decision situations the best one can expect is data-informed decision making. In this process, one examines available data and tries to see how it informs ones understanding of a situation. In a highly unstructured decision situation, an effective decision maker needs both knowledge and facts. A subjective assessment and assumption analysis becomes especially important. Decisions related to implementing digital transformation involve semistructured and unstructured decision situations.

Managers need to develop and embed processes for collecting, storing, maintaining, and analyzing data that can help answer important, recurring decision questions. Creating and managing an approach to quantitative and qualitative data use requires a sophisticated information system. A mix of people skills, technologies, and managerial procedures are needed to create information and support its timely flow to decision makers for data-driven, data-based, and data-informed decision making. Using data appropriately in decision making is key to successful digital transformation.

Need for Computerized Decision Support

In this digital era, managers realize the growing need for computerized decision support. Today decision making is challenging and the challenge to make "good" decisions is increasing. The need to make faster decisions has also increased. Too much information is common in decision situations and much of that information is often only marginally relevant. Finally, there is often more distortion of information in society. For these reasons specifically, there is an emphasis on improving data-based decision making in organizations. These reasons also create a need for more analytics and decision support.

Overall, a complex decision-making environment creates a need for computerized decision support. Decision support remains a broad concept that prescribes using computerized systems and other analytical tools to assist individuals and groups in making decisions.

Research and case studies provide evidence that a well-designed and appropriate computerized DSS can encourage data-based decisions, improve decision quality, and improve the efficiency and effectiveness of decision processes.

Most managers want more analysis and they want specific decision relevant reports quickly. Certainly, managers have many and increasing information needs. Effective decision support provides managers more independence to retrieve and analyze data and documents to obtain facts and results when they need them.

From a different perspective, cognitive decision making biases exist and create a need for decision support. Information presentation and information availability influence decision makers both positively and negatively. Reducing bias has been a secondary motivation for providing analytics and decision support. Most managers accept that some people are biased decision makers, but likely wonder if proposed analytics and decision support would reduce bias. Decision makers do "anchor" on the initial information they receive and that behavior influences how they interpret subsequent information. In addition, decision makers tend to place the greatest attention on more recent information and either ignore or forget historical information. The evidence is convincing that these and other biases can alter decisions.

Changing decision making environments, managerial requests, and decision maker limitations create a need for more and better decision support. We should consider building a computerized decision support when two conditions exist: (1) Good data/information is likely to improve the quality of decisions, (2) potential decision support users recognize a need for and want to use technology to support their data-based decision making needs.

Key Skills of Data-Based Decision Makers

Decision making habits are often learned by trial and error. Decision making skills should be learned through more deliberate, systematic effort. Culture can promote the use of data to make decisions or be neutral on this topic. More data and easier to use analytical tools provide an opportunity for improving operational decision making, but many managers must learn new behaviors and skills to actually use data and analyses effectively. Generally, managers must expand their skill sets to use data and analysis effectively. Data-based decision making requires a specialized skill set in addition to other decision making skills.

Organizations that embrace measurement have a data-centric culture. This encourages and rewards managers for making decisions based on meaningful data, rather than solely based on intuition, cf., Kanter (2013). Managers must enhance and refine their understanding of the possibilities of data analysis. Managers must strive to understand the meaning of frequently used analyses. Also, managers must be rewarded for incorporating results of data and analysis into their thinking about a situation.

Shea, Santos, and Byrnes (2012) differentiate between data-driven and data supported decisions. They note both processes use quantitative and qualitative data to inform and make decisions. Supposedly data-supported decisions "use the same data but they also take into account people, issues, ethics, and broader system effects." They caution that an excessive "data driven" emphasis can contribute to ethical blind spots poor decisions. Data-based decision making can and should incorporate ethics and ethical decision making.

Using data and analyses is sometimes challenging. Rob Enderle (2013; 2014), a technology analyst, provides examples of what he considered poor use of data and analyses at IBM, Microsoft, and Siemens. For example, he reports Microsoft's internal market research organization was providing executives with "results that made decisions they had already made look smarter." Hindsight can suggest data distortion and misuse, but based on his personal experience he observed "a surprisingly small number of the companies that sell analytics tools actually rely on those tools for major decisions."

Blogger Kalie Moore (2014) at Business Intelligence software vendor datapine.com raises a similar issue. She writes "insights we provide are completely useless if, at the end of the day, these reports are ignored by the actual decision makers." Moore felt business leaders were not using data in decision making for three reasons: (1) overreliance on past experience, (2) going with their gut and cooking the data, and (3) cognitive biases. These are serious concerns. There are ways to overcome biased behavior, but managers must become aware of their own biases and the problem resulting from specific biases. Managers must develop reflective skills, especially regarding biases in data use, to become effective data-based decision makers. Reflective skills means *thinking about or reflecting on what you do.*

Data analyses can be used to bolster and provide biased confirmation of previously made decisions. Also, analyses can be requested that support biased rationalizing of decisions. Skilled data-based decision makers must learn to *reserve judgment and postpone a final choice until the available facts are presented and evaluated.* A decision should then be made that incorporates and reconciles the facts.

So what are the specialized data analytics decision skills managers and decision makers need? The primary skills seem to broadly encompass: (1) collecting and identifying relevant data, (2) using software to perform statistical analysis including charting of data, (3) interpreting data and analyses in the context of an actual decision situation, and (4) using analyses of data, including sensitivity analyses, to inform decisions. Let's review these skills briefly.

1. Collecting and identifying relevant data. Organizations collect large amounts of data and external data can also be purchased. Often new data can also be captured. Managers need to understand data resources and data capture and how to work with stored data, to use metadata, to identify what data is available and what new data should be captured.

2. Using software to perform statistical analysis including charting of data. Often desktop tools like Excel and Tableau are adequate. Learning a statistical analysis package helps decision makers interpret analytical results and understand limitations of statistical analysis.

3. Interpreting data and analyses in the context of an actual decision situation. Decision makers need to match data and analyses to questions of interest. Many decisions can be framed either in terms of gains or losses. How a decision is framed can also impact choices. Decision makers should ask: What do I need to know about this situation? Is there data that will help me understand my choices in

the situation? What does the data mean? Do I have a pre-conceived solution or biases?

4. Using analyses of data, including sensitivity analyses, to inform decisions. Data can inform decisions, but data does not always provide conclusive evidence. In some situations data analysis shows a strong correlation, but the causal evidence is much more circumstantial. Rather than ignoring data, managers should show caution when they use available data. Correlation is not causation, but in many cases correlation is the strongest conclusion about a relationship.

Many observers agree quantitative skills are important to data-based decision making.

Until recently, data analysis skills were primarily taught to statisticians, market researchers, actuaries and other specialists more than to people planning careers as managers. Times have changed and teaching applied data analysis skills is increasingly popular. Top International Business Schools are addressing this managerial skills gap. There is broad recognition that managers and decision makers need to be skilled data users and data interpreters. Managers need to be skilled at data-based decision making.

Using data and analyzing data is every manager's job. If that goal is to be realized, then current and future decision makers must develop and enhance skills needed to use data effectively. Rationalizing before a decision is made or afterward is equally inappropriate. A skilled, data-based decision maker follows a process that begins with asking the right questions, and then answering the question using facts, relevant data and analyses prior to making a decision.

Steps to Develop Data-Based Decision Support

Encouraging and developing data-based decision support is an organizationwide effort and requires many resources, including people, money, and technologies. Building an effective enterprisewide decision support capability can help improve decision making, but meeting that goal is a challenging task. Providing companywide decision support requires creating a sophisticated information technology architecture of computing assets. That architecture provides the foundation for data-based decision making and digital transformation. Data-based decision making benefits from computer-based support for collecting, analyzing, and sharing different types of data. Often relevant decision support information is derived from real-time and historical quantitative and qualitative data.

Creating and managing a modern computing architecture requires a mix of people skills, technologies, and managerial procedures that are often difficult to assemble and implement. For example, storing a large quantity of decision support data is likely to require Cloud deployments and purchasing the latest hardware and software. Many companies need to purchase high-end servers and advanced database systems, including NoSQL databases such as MongoDB, Cassandra, and CouchDB, and possibly translytical databases that support real-time transaction processing and data analytics. To implement a decision support architecture an organization also needs people with advanced database design and data management skills.

How can managers increase the chances of a successful data-based decision support implementation? After evaluating some alternate suggestions, we have concluded that once an appropriate need has been identified, then the following steps can help create, implement, and promote use of data-based decision support in decision-making processes, see Figure 3.2.

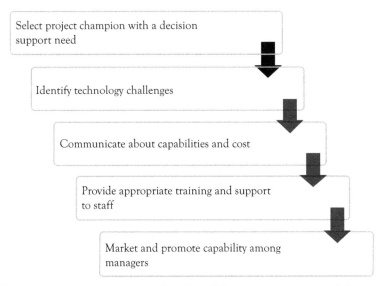

Figure 3.2 Steps to create a data-based decision support capability

In Figure 3.2, the first step is to identify an influential project champion with a decision support need. The project champion must be a respected, senior manager. A project champion can deal with political issues and help insure that everyone realizes they are part of an analytics and decision support team. Managers need to stay focused on a company's decision support development goals.

Second, managers should be prepared for technology shortfalls. Technology problems are inevitable with data-oriented decision support projects. Often the technology to accomplish a desired decision support task is not currently available or is not easily implemented. Unforeseen problems and frustrations will occur.

The third step is to tell everyone as much as you can about the costs of creating and using the proposed decision support capability. Managers need to know how much it costs to develop, access, and analyze decision support data.

Fourth, be sure to invest in training. Set aside adequate resources, both time and money, so users can learn to access and leverage the new decision support capability.

Finally, market and promote the new capability to the managers you want to use the system. Provide incentive and motivation for appropriate use of the system. Managers must be aware of a new capability and must want to use it.

Effective decision support requires ongoing innovation and refinement. As decisions become more complex and as data increases in quantity and variety, systems must be refined and enhanced. Decision support requires an iterative development process, executing the steps in Figure 3.2 repetitively.

Find an Opportunity to Create Competitive Advantage

Managers want to create capabilities that provide a competitive advantage. Decision support, analytics, and business intelligence can provide advantage, but the mere existence of a capability does not create sustainable advantage. According to Setia et al. (2013, p. 583) "the relative ubiquity of digital technologies implies that merely investing in digital technologies or enhancing their usage may not be sufficient for a firm to gain competitive advantage." The real value comes from understanding how a proposed capability may provide advantage. This knowledge is crucial for evaluating opportunities. Also, it is important to assess how likely it is that a successful implementation will provide advantage. At an abstract level based on Barney (1991), technologists need to ask if the novel capability is valuable, rare, inimitable, and nonsubstitutable. Then establish whether the organization is ready to implement the capability.

A competitive advantage is a resource, capability, skill, or characteristic of an organization that significantly enhances success in a market, rivalry situation, or competitive encounter. Competitive advantage results from doing something better than competitors that create value and superior performance in a timely manner.

A proposed capability must have the potential to create real value in a realistic time frame. For example, a novel decision support capability must demonstrably improve decision-making efficiency or effectiveness or both. In general, a novel decision support capability should be hidden from competitors and it should be difficult for competitors to identify and emulate. An internal facing system used by managers is more likely to remain rare and unknown to competitors than an externally facing capability used by customers or other external stakeholders. A proposed capability must also be difficult to duplicate or imitate. Systems developed by company information technology staff are more likely to create sustainable advantage than off-the-shelf solutions purchased from a vendor. Finally, the functionality of any new capability must be difficult to duplicate if it becomes known. One hopes any substitutes for the capability have serious limitations.

Decision support and analytics may and can create competitive advantage. A decision support capability is a competitive advantage when it is (1) a major strength, (2) unique and proprietary, and (3) sustainable long enough to realize a payback. Digital transformation and improved decision support may not create a competitive advantage—it depends on the vision, competitor actions, timing, and implementation.

Barney's resource-based view of a firm suggests questions that should be asked when vendors or internal advocates are promoting any capability as a potential competitive advantage.

- Will the proposed capability create significant value?
- Is the proposed capability novel and rare?
- Is the proposed capability difficult to copy, duplicate, or imitate?
- Do substitutes for the capability have limitations that will discourage using them?
- Is the organization ready to implement and exploit the proposed capability?

Decision support can create competitive advantage by significantly improving data-based decision making efficiency and effectiveness, by supporting cost and/or differentiation strategies, and by increasing organizational control, innovation, or adaptability. High risk decision support projects such as key digital transformation decision-related projects are the most likely to result in a competitive advantage or fail spectacularly. Gaining any advantage may require large financial investments and be temporary. Some decision support development opportunities are better than others. Many very useful decision support capabilities will not provide a significant competitive advantage, but the capabilities are needed to remain competitive in the industry. Evidence about the need and potential value of a proposed capability can help choose among opportunities.

Some software vendors claim a specific "new" application will provide a competitive advantage. Supposedly organizations that implement a vendor's solution will gain a competitive advantage. This broad promise sounds too good to be true, so don't believe the promise. Ask questions, get answers and facts, tailor and customize off-the-shelf applications.

Summary

More efficient and effective managerial decision making is difficult to achieve in an increasingly complex, data intensive, digital business ecosystem. Stakeholders, including shareholders, senior management, customers, and partners, have high expectations for better results and continue to want more value.

Increasing and improving data-based decision making is key to successfully implementing a digital transformation vision. Some people advocate for data-driven decision making, others for data-based or data-informed decision making. These approaches differ and each can provide value in the right situation. Data are important and decision making should incorporate facts, but often assumptions and opinions should also influence choices. Managers need to learn new analytical skills and an organization's culture should reward data-based decision making. Overall, complex decision-making environments create a need for computerized decision support and for more sophisticated decision making.

Using data-based decision making provides a generalized opportunity to create an advantage as part of a digital transformation strategy. In general, managers should use data-based decision making for semistructured decision situations. Managers should use all relevant data in semistructured situations, and should consider ethical issues, values, situational factors, assumptions, and other less tangible factors. This factual, data-based approach is especially important in assessing digital transformation opportunities.

CHAPTER 4

Analytics and High-Velocity Decision Making

Managers must match the velocity of streaming data with high-velocity, data-based decision making and agile execution to successfully compete.[1] Digital transformation is ongoing and evolving. Managers engaged in finding ways to make greater use of digital data must understand the importance of analyzing and using digital data in decision making to actually improve the overall functioning and success of an organization. Digital transformation maturity refers to the progress of managers in implementing various actions to re-imagine or re-invent the business, typically leveraging technology. Managers implementing a digital transformation strategy should focus on adopting and using innovative technology that can enhance organizational decision-making capabilities.

In a collaborative research study conducted by MIT Sloan Management Review and Deloitte professional services network, Kane et al. (2015) found that among digitally maturing organizations, nearly 90 percent of strategies focus on improving decisions and innovation. The following six sections emphasize improving decision making and include: (1) the basics of analytics, (2) current trends in advanced analytics and applications, (3) a guide to identify and select data analytics tools, (4) analytics as an enabler for data-based decision making, (5) high-velocity decision making, and (6) the ethical challenges encountered with data analytics and data-based decision making.

---

[1] Dykes, B. 2017. "Big Data: Forget Volume and Variety, Focus On Velocity." *Forbes*, June 28. https://forbes.com/sites/brentdykes/2017/06/28/big-data-forget-volume-and-variety-focus-on-velocity/#5de2336f7d67

Basics of Analytics

Analytics is often described as the science of analysis and discovery. The term refers to quantitative analysis of data. People who conduct analyses and develop analytic applications are decision or data scientists. Analytics refers to a broad set of tools and capabilities that provide decision support. Analytic capabilities are important in data-driven and model-driven DSS and analysis with quantitative and statistical tools is the focus of special studies such as knowledge discovery or data mining.

Davenport and Harris (2007) define analytics as "extensive use of data, statistical and quantitative analysis, exploratory and predictive models, and fact-based management to drive decisions and actions. The analytics may be input for human decisions or drive fully automated decisions" (p. 7).

Analytics is a broad umbrella term that includes business analytics and data analytics. Business analytics (BA) use data and analytics to improve business operations and decision making. BA includes optimization, Artificial Intelligence (AI) and Machine Learning (ML). Data analytics applies quantitative and statistical methods to analyze large, complex organizational data sets. Managers need to understand the value of using data analytics and the decision support capabilities made possible by leveraging data.

Analytic applications have three main technology features: (1) data management and retrieval, (2) mathematical and statistical analysis and models, and (3) techniques for data visualization and display. Analytic applications are used to process large amounts of structured and unstructured data to find patterns and provide information. Analyzing data can be challenging and more data can increase the complexity of an analysis. More data does not mean better analytics. Like all computerized systems, for analytics to be useful the data must be accurate, complete, and representative of the real world.

Some sources consider analytics as a subset of business intelligence (BI), while some use the terms analytics and BI interchangeably, other commentators are more specific and consider only reporting analytics as another name for BI. In this discussion, data-driven DSS and BI are considered as reporting analytic applications. There are three major types of analytics: (1) reporting analytics, (2) prescriptive analytics, and (3) predictive analytics.

Information Systems vendors and analysts tend to use BI as a category of software tools that can be used to extract and analyze data from corporate databases. The most common BI software is query and reporting tools. This software extracts data from a database and creates formatted reports.

Prescriptive analytics manipulate large data sets to make recommendations. This type of decision support prescribes or recommends an action, rather than a forecast or a summary report. Prescriptive analysis relies on sophisticated analytics including graph analysis, simulations and machine learning. Through evaluating decision options, managers can use prescriptive analytics to take advantage of an opportunity in the future. Using What… questions such as "What should be done to achieve xxx in the future?" Prescriptive analytics is based on quantitative and statistical models and this category of analytics includes model-driven DSS.

Predictive analytics is a general term for using simple and complex models to support anticipatory decision making. Analysis of historical data is used to build a predictive model to support a specific decision task. The decision task may be determining who to target in a marketing campaign, what products to stock, possibility of fraud, or who the "best" customers are for a firm. Using historical data, predictor variables are identified for building quantitative or business rule models. The model makes a prediction for a decision task.

Managers in consumer-packaged goods, banking, gambling, energy, and health care industries are the most active users of predictive analytics. Predictive analytics is increasingly incorporated in day-to-day operations management tasks. New projects can be implemented faster because software has improved for analysis and development, but the number of IT professionals skilled in using the many varied analytical techniques is inadequate to meet the demand.

Developing analytics should involve both business and IT managers. This joint development process should help in understanding and in some cases automating business operations decisions. Creating a meaningful analytics development partnership can facilitate improved and enhanced routine decision making. Working together on analytics development can serve as a bridge between IT and business managers.

Development and use of analytics should be a core technology competency of many companies and managers should be reluctant to outsource or offshore the capability. Managers must realize the cost of each analytics project is an investment in building competency and it can also reduce operations costs and enhance operations. Certainly there is a learning curve associated with analytics but consultants can reduce the curve. Managers should not however assume that programmers outside their firm can easily understand the peculiarities and needs of their business. As organizations capture more and more data, it will be important to analyze and use the data to enhance business results. Implementing analytics is NOT just another routine Information Technology (IT) project.

Based on a number of sources including the IBM Analytics Quotient (AQ) quiz, the following questions and responses identify best practices for using IT to implement analytics.

Answering the questions presented in Table 4.1 can provide managers with a baseline guide to assess current development of analytics capabilities.

A joint MIT Sloan Management Review and IBM report identified three core competencies organizations must master to achieve a competitive advantage with analytics. The first is information management, which focuses on standardized data practices. The second is analytics skills, which rely on core discipline expertise, built on robust tools. Finally, there must exist a data-centric culture that sees analytics as a key asset to support evidence-based management.

Disruption is continuing and perhaps accelerating. Analytics are important decision support tools that lead to data-based decision making.

Current Trends in Advanced Analytics and Its Applications

Analytics and business intelligence (BI) technologies continue to be key enablers of most organizational data and decision support strategies. The opportunities for mobile BI are many, and the trends toward self-service

Table 4.1 Decision guide for implementing analytics

Ask questions	Guideline
1. What types of data sources should managers analyze?	In general, standard enterprise data sources across functions should be combined with data from external sources, point of sale, RFID, and social media
2. How important is the quality of data used in analyses?	**Very important.** An organization should have an enterprise data model. Common master data and metadata must exist and strong data governance practices must be in place
3. Should managers document outcomes of analytics initiatives?	**Yes.** Managers should initiate a documentation process to capture how the use of business analytics has changed business operations. Successful projects will lead to more projects
4. How important is using predictive models?	**Very important.** Integrated planning and predictive modeling can enable an organization to adjust policy and execution in response to shifting dynamics in the organization and business environment
5. How should managers assess and manage risk?	Risk metrics should be industry specific. Managers should share risk management assessment and mitigation processes across the organization, identify the most significant cross-departmental risks in an effort to reduce loss, and link risk reduction and specific risks to business objectives and improved performance
6. Should managers centralize resources for performing and developing analytics?	**Yes, but** analytics knowledge should be widespread throughout an organization. Using analytics should become part of the organizational culture. Managers should establish an analytics center of excellence and cross functional analytics team
7. What general analytics solutions should be implemented in organizations?	Solutions are in four categories: (1) Reporting and analytics, (2) Planning, budgeting and forecasting, (3) Predictive and advanced analytics, and (4) Governance, risk and compliance analytics
8. How should managers anticipate future events and results?	It is important to use both qualitative and quantitative methods, including: (1) experience and intuition, (2) predictive analytics for priority needs, (3) "what if" scenarios, and (4) integrated planning and predictive models

analytics and visualization are both exciting and promising for data-centric organizations.

BI and related technology initiatives attract a lot of attention from technology experts, managers, consultants, and vendors. A recent survey of BI professionals identified data discovery/visualization, self-service BI, and data quality/master data management as the most important trends. In her Datapine blog, Mona Lebied (2016) identified key areas for BI and analytics ranging from security and digitization to cloud analytics, embedded BI, and data storytelling.

Artificial Intelligence (AI) and Machine Learning (ML) are also attracting attention. Managers in many organizations are trying to understand AI in general and the possibilities for their business. Gartner has flagged advanced AI and ML as important trends for organizations by 2018. AI is a broad concept that has been around for many years. AI refers to the simulation of "smart" behaviors in computers. ML is a subset of AI that uses algorithms to learn and improve from experience. The opportunities for these technologies in business and health care are extensive. In a recent Forbes article, Marr (2017) highlights disease identification and diagnosis, crowd sourcing treatment options and drug response monitoring and disease surveillance, as areas where AI is having significant impacts in the health domain. Smart cities, smart manufacturing and smart cars are also capturing public attention.

Core to generating new value from decision support and analytics, managers should experiment with and explore new opportunities in AI/ML, visual data discovery, and data storytelling. Moving beyond traditional graphs and charts, this era of infographics pushes boundaries in terms of trying new ways to use data to tell a business story through the effective use of sophisticated approaches to data visualization.

Collaborative decision support is fostered through the increased availability and use of mobile technology and Web 2.0 technologies. BI is no longer solely for senior. Self-service BI provides opportunities to share data. Also, improvements in software facilitate new ways for embedding decision support features in existing software applications.

With increasing investment of resources in data and technology and heightened expectations for digital transformation, we anticipate many organizations will establish dedicated centers for analytics and self-service BI (cf. Lebeid 2016).

Data governance and security are high priorities for most organizations. Security is a consideration for managers in all businesses looking at cloud analytics and cloud storage options. While self-service BI in the cloud affords many benefits to individual users, realizing this level of flexibility and agility is challenging in terms of security and data governance (Potter 2015).

Analyzing data is often challenging and more data can increase the complexity of an analysis. More data does not mean better analysis. Hiring data scientists, buying more hardware or software or hiring consultants does not guarantee success. It may be necessary to implement capabilities like in-memory processing or software like Hadoop. Additional training is probably needed and possibly new staff might also be needed.

McKinsey director David Court (2012) argued multiple success factors must be present to use new technologies: creative use of internal and external data, developing workable models, and transforming the company to take advantage of data. Finally, Court notes "you've got to make a decision support tool the frontline user understands and has confidence in."

To exploit these trends six critical success factors must be present: (1) managers must want to use analytics and decision support, (2) knowledgeable and innovative data and decision support analysts, (3) high quality data, (4) accurate models for forecasting and prediction, (5) appropriate technology, and (6) data-centric culture.

Select Analytics Tools and Technologies

Selecting the most appropriate analytics approach and tools for a specific task or project is important. The approach that is the best fit depends upon many factors including: (1) the need and objective, (2) data availability, (3) training and background of current data analysts, (4) vendor support, and (5) the industry/type of organization. Choosing the wrong approach and tools often results in a difficult and incorrect analysis. Analytics is about asking specific questions and finding the best answers. As discussed in a previous chapter, a question asking technique should also be used for choosing analytics approaches and tools.

Descriptive analytics primarily uses data aggregation and statistical tools like averages and differences. Predictive analytics use more complex statistical models like regression and correlation and forecasting techniques like moving averages. Diagnostic analytics uses tools like drill down, interactive data visualization and data mining. Finally, prescriptive analytics uses tools like optimization, simulation, scenario analysis, and case-based reasoning.

In a Forbes article, Bernard Marr (2016) sets out six approaches to analytics. In considering these approaches it is important to understand when specific tools should be used. We have briefly assessed these approaches in terms of the nature of the data needed and the business goal(s) that can be met. The following is our assessment.

1. Business Experiments

Testing ideas is often a goal of data analytics. A business experiment approach is used to test the validity of an idea. This may be a strategic hypothesis, a new product package or a marketing campaign. Davenport (2009) advocates a "test and learn" approach to conducting business experiments noting that experiment design is key to generating a sound evidence base. We recommend using a business experiment approach when seeking to test ideas systematically.

2. Causal Analysis

Finding causes helps understand a situation so changes or prediction is possible. Regression is a primary causal analysis tool that is useful when understanding and/or prediction is required and adequate data are available on plausible predictor variables. Regression is a statistical tool for investigating the relationship between variables. For example, managers might use regression analysis to understand the causal relationship between price and product demand. Use causal analysis when a complex situation is data rich and managers want better understanding.

3. Correlation Analysis

This is a statistical technique that allows managers to determine whether there is a relationship between two separate variables. It also helps to determine the strength of the relationship between the variables. We might use correlation analysis to understand if there is a relationship between positive customer experience and customers sensitivity to changes in the price of a product or service. Use correlation analysis to explore relationships.

4. *Forecasting Analysis*

This approach uses a time series of data values to forecast or predict other values. For example, managers may use sales data from the past to predict future sales values. Perform a forecasting analysis when the primary goal is estimation of a variable(s) of interest at some specified future date.

5. *Scenario Analysis*

Managers can consider "what-if" questions by analyzing a variety of possible future events or scenarios considering possible alternate outcomes (Power and Heavin 2017). Use scenario analysis where there are numerous possible course of action and a high degree of uncertainty about the potential outcome.

6. *Visual Analytics*

Data can be analyzed in many ways and the simplest way is to create a visual or graph as a means of identifying patterns or trends. This is an interdisciplinary approach integrating data analysis with data visualization and human interaction. For example, a sales manager could use an interactive map to better understand customer purchasing behaviors by region. Use data visualization when managers are interested in directly deriving insights from large volumes of data.

As mentioned previously, business analytics and data analytics are terms used interchangeably to describe a systematic process of purposefully examining and using data sets with statistical and quantitative models, and leveraging the capabilities of sophisticated algorithms and technologies. Often the goal is to draw conclusions about the underlying meaning or implications of the data. Business analytics emphasizes business uses of analytics, while data analytics has a broader focus across organizations and settings. There is no single best approach for meeting every analysis goal. Once the most appropriate analytics approach for a specific situation is selected, a manager or analyst must select analytics tools and technologies to conduct the analysis. There are many analytics and decision support software tools available and many of them are open source and widely available. Managers should consider and evaluate the technologies currently available and the technical capabilities of staff available in-house before going to the market for new software tools or to hire experts.

Managers and analysts continue to investigate new opportunities in visual data discovery and data storytelling (Heavin and Power 2017). Moving beyond traditional graphs and charts, sophisticated data visualization technologies promote new ways of telling a business story from data insights to data visualization. Analytics approaches are evolving.

Analytics Should Inform Data-Based Decision Making

Analytics is an integral component of a successful organizational digital transformation strategy. Use of analytics can offer individuals, organizations, governments, and our global society "data-based" perspectives on existing challenges and possible solutions. Analytics can provide facts to improve data-based decision making and help find meaning in an increasingly complex environment.

In her Teradata blog, Yasmeen Ahmad (2016) identified advantages of analytics, including: (1) increased proactivity and the ability to anticipate needs, (2) delivering the right products and services at the right time, (3) improved personalization and service, and (4) optimizing and improving the customer experience. Analytics provide these benefits when incorporated in data-based decision processes. Analytics has been lauded by some as the "silver bullet" solution to finding an organizational competitive advantage. Sadly, it is NOT a "silver bullet," but rather analytics is more like the raw unformed silver! Gaining Ahmad's advantages does seem reasonable, but the task is an ongoing challenge.

Data albeit "good data" on its own will not result in good decision making (cf. Shah et al. 2012). In their study of data-savvy practitioners, Shah and colleagues identify five challenges to data-based decision making in organizations, these include:

1. Few employees have analytical skills;
2. IT departments need to invest more resources in providing information and less in the technology aspect of IT;
3. There is broad acknowledgment good quality data exist, however it is often a challenge to locate important data sources;

4. Managing data and providing information is widely perceived as the sole responsibility of the IT function. Traditionally, business managers did not engage in data and information management. The typical manager often neglects understanding information that is received.

5. There is an urgent need to develop more informed sceptics. "Employees need to recognize that not all numbers are created equal—some are more reliable than others."

Notably, the Shah et al. study highlights the widespread misperception that analytics is the responsibility of an organization's IT function. Analytics is the everyone's responsibility, it should "put information in the hands of business analysts and business users and offer significant potential to create business value and competitive advantage" (Jones 2016).

Benefits of analytics are always constrained or limited by the manager or managers who use the results to make decisions. In order to achieve meaningful integration between analytics tools and technologies, analytics must support and reinforce data-based decision making and management. Key performance data should be included in a data-based management process that provides routine evaluations to improve organizational outcomes, including quality, and financial metrics. This integrated more holistic and balanced view of providing analytics is illustrated in Figure 4.1.

Negotiating the balance between an organization's approach to data analytics and a data-based management strategy can be difficult. To achieve this dual focus, it is essential that managers participate in the

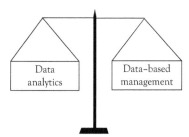

Figure 4.1 Finding a balance between "Data analytics" and "Data-based management"

process of analyzing data in a way that leverages new data insights and integrates them into the organization's management and decision-making processes. Shah et al. (2012) suggest that managers need to be better trained to use new analytics tools, paying particular attention to building analytics into managerial processes. If a balance is not achieved, managers run the risk of investing in expensive analytics technologies that are not used by managers. It is important to implement the "right" amount of analytics to support a data-centric culture and that should lead to better data-based decision making.

High-Velocity Decision Making

Consequential decisions can and often should be made using a high-velocity, high-quality decision-making process. High-velocity decision making is a new label for a familiar idea: make reversible decisions using streamlined, rapid data-based decision processes focused on issues, yet make sure the processes are thoughtful and goal-oriented. Jeff Bezos, Founder and CEO of Amazon.com, Inc., in his 2016 and 2017 shareholder letters discusses decisions and decision making. His ideas are very relevant to managers interested in using analytics and decision support to improve decision making outcomes. In this era of digital transformation, Bezos advocates for using high-velocity, high-quality decision making for consequential and *reversible* decisions. The following paragraphs explain the rules of high-velocity decision making:

Rule 1: Know what kind of decision you are trying to make. Is it a Type 1 consequential and irreversible decision? or a Type 2 changeable and reversible decision?

Bezos notes **Type 1** decisions are

consequential and irreversible or nearly irreversible—one-way doors—and these decisions must be made methodically, carefully, slowly, with great deliberation and consultation. If you walk through and don't like what you see on the other side, you can't get back to where you were before.

Type 2 decisions are different.

Most decisions are changeable, reversible—they're two-way doors. If you've made a suboptimal Type 2 decision, you don't have to live with the consequences for that long. You can reopen the door and go back through. Type 2 decisions can and should be made quickly by high judgment individuals or small groups.[2]

Bezos argues

As organizations get larger, there seems to be a tendency to use the heavy-weight Type 1 decision making process on most decisions, including many Type 2 decisions. The end result of this is slowness, unthoughtful risk aversion, failure to experiment sufficiently, and consequently diminished invention.[3]

Rule 2: Strive to be a Day 1 company.
Bezos explains

I've been reminding people that it's Day 1 for a couple of decades. I work in an Amazon building named Day 1, and when I moved buildings, I took the name with me. I spend time thinking about this topic. ... Day 2 is stasis. Followed by irrelevance. Followed by excruciating, painful decline. Followed by death. And that is why it is always Day 1. .....

Day 2 companies make *high-quality* decisions, but they make high-quality decisions slowly. To keep the energy and dynamism of Day 1, you have to somehow make high-quality, *high-velocity*

---

[2] **Note**: We assume a "high judgment" individual is a person with experience and good judgment.

[3] **Bezos** "The opposite situation is less interesting and there is undoubtedly some survivorship bias. Any companies that habitually use the light-weight Type 2 decision-making process to make Type 1 decisions go extinct before they get large."

decisions. Easy for start-ups and very challenging for large organizations. The senior team at Amazon is determined to keep our decision making velocity high. Speed matters in business—plus a high-velocity decision making environment is more fun too.

Rule 3: Strive to make high-quality, high-velocity decisions.

Never use a one-size-fits-all decision making process. Many decisions are reversible, two-way doors. Those decisions can use a light-weight process. For those, so what if you're wrong?

Rule 4: Consider the trade-off between seeking more information and a slower decision.

Most decisions should probably be made with somewhere around 70 percent of the information you wish you had. If you wait for 90 percent, in most cases, you're probably being slow. Plus, either way, you need to be good at quickly recognizing and correcting bad decisions. If you're good at course correcting, being wrong may be less costly than you think, whereas being slow is going to be expensive for sure.

Rule 5: Disagree and commit when appropriate for Type 2 decisions. Trust other managers and know when to respectfully disagree and go along with the group.
The phrase "disagree and commit" will save a lot of time.

If you have conviction on a particular direction even though there's no consensus, it's helpful to say, "Look, I know we disagree on this but will you gamble with me on it? Disagree and commit?" By the time you're at this point, no one can know the answer for sure, and you'll probably get a quick yes.

Rule 6: Go for quick escalation. Know when senior management should make the decision.

Recognize true misalignment issues early and escalate them immediately. Sometimes teams have different objectives and fundamentally different views. They are not aligned. No amount of discussion, no number of meetings will resolve that deep misalignment. Without escalation, the default dispute resolution mechanism for this scenario is exhaustion. Whoever has more stamina carries the decision.

Know when a decision needs to be escalated to the senior team. As Bezos concludes "'You've worn me down' is an awful decision making process. It's slow and de-energizing. Go for quick escalation instead—it's better."

Rule 7: Strive to have the spirit and the heart of a small company. Bezos asks

Have you settled only for decision quality, or are you mindful of decision velocity too? Are the world's trends tailwinds for you? Are you falling prey to proxies, or do they serve you? And most important of all, are you delighting customers? We can have the scope and capabilities of a large company and the spirit and heart of a small one. But we have to choose it.

Case studies and news stories at DSSResources.com suggest that high-velocity environments are increasingly common and that managers must learn to make high-velocity decisions if they are to remain relevant and part of the decision process. Managers must develop fast, incremental processes for Type 2 decisions in high-velocity decision environments. In some situations, those decisions should be made by software algorithms. In rapidly changing environments, people will be eliminated from some decision processes because they are too slow. Highly-structured Type 2 decisions will be automated. Also, analytics can be used to analyze and understand business data that can be used to make high-velocity decisions.

Rule 8: Strategic, consequential, irreversible Type 1 decisions should be made using a high-quality decision-making process that is methodical, careful, and thoughtful, and made with deliberation and consultation.

High-velocity decision making is not the same as high-speed decision making. High-speed decision making describes only how to make fast decisions, while high-velocity decision making means decisions are made quickly and, in a goal-oriented direction. High-velocity decision making means a decision maker is aware of and considers the goals that are being pursued. If the decision is a reversible, nonprogrammed decision about new, novel situations requiring innovation, it can be made using a high-velocity, high-quality decision-making process.

Bezos' views are similar to but do differ from results of Bourgeois and Eisenhardt's (1988) decision making research. In their classic study, Bourgeois and Eisenhardt investigated how executives make strategic decisions in industries where the rate of technological and competitive change is so extreme that market information is often unavailable or obsolete, where strategic windows are opening and shutting quickly, and where the cost of error is involuntary exit. They noted

> Our results consist of a set of paradoxes which the successful firms resolve and the unsuccessful firms do not. We found an imperative to make major decisions carefully, but to decide quickly; to have a powerful, decisive CEO and a simultaneously powerful top management team; to seek risk and innovation, but to execute a safe, incremental implementation. Despite the apparent paradox, effective firms do all of these simultaneously.

In a related study published in 1989, Eisenhardt reported that her "results link fast decisions to several factors, including the use of real-time information, multiple alternatives, counselors, consensus with qualification, and decision integration" (p. 573). She also noted "the emergent perspective highlights emotion as integral to high stakes decision making … emotion is critical for understanding strategic decision making" (p. 573).

Strategic decisions are important, usually with long-term consequences, and with large resource commitments. By definition strategic decisions are consequential and some are not reversible. Reversibility means senior managers are able to change, roll-back, and reverse a decision and that the actions to implement the decision can be undone. Rather than two states, reversible and irreversible, there seems to be a vague continuum of decision reversibility ranging from completely irreversible to completely reversible. For example, Bezos notes some decisions are "nearly irreversible."

High-velocity decision making at Amazon under Jeff Bezos is apparently effective. Making successful strategic decisions in an environment of rapid change does create paradoxes we only partially understand. One aspect of the decision process paradox is captured in the question—How do we know when and if a decision is reversible?

Ethical Challenges for Decision Making

Modern managers are becoming more strategic about the capture, storage, and value extraction from data. This strategic approach typically means leveraging large data sets to extract insightful information that was previously unknown. These insights are used to maintain or create competitive advantage for the organization. Analytics may provide results to identify new markets, new products and services, opportunities to grow revenue, and opportunities to drive down costs with the end goal of boosting organizational performance. These new uses of data are creating ethical challenges.

For example, the general data protection regulation (GDPR) in Europe and significant differences in data protection legislation across jurisdictions has stimulated much discussion about data privacy, security and protection by government agencies, regulatory bodies and managers in both public and private organizations. This ongoing discussion is widely underpinned by ethical scenarios in business related to IT. Ethics refers to "moral rules, codes, or principles which provide guidelines for right and truthful behavior in specific situations" (Lewis 1985, p. 382). The areas of analytics, BI, decision support, and big data are relatively new, we continue to uncover new and increasingly complex ethical questions on a regular basis.

Some people think that building and using a computerized decision support and analytics capability is ethically neutral. That view is poorly informed and incorrect. People are faced with ethical choices when dealing with computerized decision support that we are only beginning to recognize, consider and evaluate. Using a stakeholder perspective illustrated in Figure 4.2, Asadi et al. (2016) consider three main stakeholders when

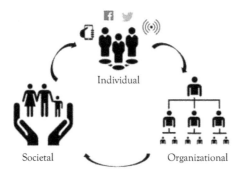

Figure 4.2 Analytics Stakeholders

evaluating the ethical implications of analytics. These stakeholders include (1) individuals who use social media, (2) organizations who capture, store and manage data, and (3) society. The societal impacts are significant as governments and industry associations struggle to regulate and create policies for emergent and rapidly changing markets (Asadi et al. 2016).

Given the multi-stakeholder perspective presented in Figure 4.2, the ethical considerations associated with analytics and decision support are complex. While technology is neutral, the decisions that people make about how technology is used to capture, store, analyze, and share data are not ethically neutral. IBM Engineer Mandy Chessell (2014) proposes nine categories of questions that should be considered by individuals and organizations when tackling ethical issues, related to data and technology including:

1. **Context**: Why was the data originally collected? How is the data now being used? How far removed from the original context is its new use? Is this a fair and appropriate use of this data?
2. **Consent and Choice**: What are the choices given to all stakeholders involved? Do they know they are making a choice? Do they really understand what they are agreeing to? Do they really have an opportunity to decline? What alternatives are offered?
3. **Reasonable:** Is the data used and the relationships derived appropriate and reasonable given the purpose it was collected for?
4. **Substantiated**: Are the sources of data used suitable, respected, complete, and timely for the application?

5. **Ownership:** Who owns the new insights generated as a result of data analysis? What are the owners' responsibilities?

6. **Fair:** How fair are the results of the application to all stakeholders affected? Is everyone properly compensated?

7. **Considered consequences:** What are the potential consequences of the data collection and analysis?

8. **Access:** What access to data is given to the data subject?

9. **Accountable:** How are mistakes and unintended consequences detected and repaired? Can the interested parties check the results that affect them?

Exploring plausible critical ethical incidents that may be faced by managers, data scientists, and other users can help understand the complexity of ethical decision making. So what situations might occur? Using Chessell's questions, please contemplate the scenarios in Table 4.2:

Table 4.2 Scenarios for data-based decisions with ethical implications

Scenario 1: A builder of a BI solution chooses not to include a key metric because the data are hard to capture and display. Eventually that missing metric, for example the weight of a prototype airplane, becomes a critical flaw that leads to major cost overruns.
Scenario 2: A sponsor proposes combining individual sales affinity card and credit score data and a software developer becomes concerned that the privacy rights of customers will be in jeopardy. The sponsor is a powerful figure in the company who does not like dissent.
Scenario 3: A software developer realizes the quality of data for a proposed data analytics solution is flawed and inaccurate and still proceeds to build the system. The system is never really used because of complaints of poor data quality.
Scenario 4: A software development team fails to validate a forecast model in an automated inventory replenishment system and managers report large inventory problems. The company takes a major write-down on obsolete inventory.
Scenario 5: A manager/user of a data-driven DSS notices a sales problem in a store and drills down into the underlying data and sees a large transaction by her husband. The manager confronts her spouse with the information he found using the system.
Scenario 6: A manager fails to use an investment management and control system in a timely manner and a subordinate makes a large, unauthorized trade. The trade is ill-advised and significant losses result.
Scenario 7: The knowledge base for a knowledge-driven DSS derived with AI and ML seems out of date and no one acts to fix the problem. The recommendations of the system become increasingly error prone and erratic. Managers start ignoring the results.

As a thought exercise ask yourself: What would you do in each situation? Why would you take that action? Who is the responsible party? Is the situation avoidable?

In many of these situations we encounter an ethical dilemma. Initially the situation seems clear cut, but other scenarios are gray and they require additional information, investigation, and even some expert advice.

Principles and values play an important role in making many significant organizational decisions. When analytics and decision support solutions are constructed, software developers make assumptions that can have ethical impacts on user choices. Also, some decisions are considered so value-laden that many people would be uncomfortable with developing decision support to assist a decision maker. One cannot specify all of the ethical issues that might be relevant to a specific decision support proposal, but once a proposal reaches the feasibility stage, the project sponsor needs to specifically address the ethical issues associated with the project. Also, during development developers need to be sensitive to how representations like charts and tables that are designed to present information impact a decision maker.

Privacy concerns are also easy to ignore during the evaluation of a analytics proposal. In many societies, people expect that certain personal and behavioral information about them will be kept private. This information belongs to the person and does not belong to a company, the public, or the government. Managers must ensure that data used in the organization does not infringe on the privacy rights if individuals. The exact extent of privacy rights for employees, customers, and other data providers is not always clearly defined. In general, unless there is a clearly compelling reason to risk violating an individual's privacy, the "fence" to protect privacy of data should be higher and larger than any minimum requirements.

The following potential analytics and decision support ethical issues require more thought: (1) data quality assurance, (2) hidden data capture, (3) propagating data errors, (4) ongoing use of obsolete decision support, (5) data mashups, data linking, and data fracking, (6) combining internal and external data sources, (7) inappropriate use of customer profiles/data, (8) legal liability issues from failing to use or from misuse of a decision support capability, (9) data/key metrics exclusion, (10) analytics/decision support model validation, (11) unauthorized data transfers, (12) lack of policies or poor policy enforcement, and (13) invasion of personal privacy. Organization policies and National and Local laws should guide the behavior of managers and developers on these and related topics.

We want to encourage and promote open discussion and proactive behavior to insure ethical use and construction of analytics and computerized decision support. To do so we need to explore the subtleties of a wide variety of ethical situations that managers, developers, and system users might encounter. When in doubt about the ethical use of a decision support or analytics tool or the need to use decision support or the consequences of poor design decisions on the behavior of decision makers, do **not** ignore the question, rather ask others, consult, and discuss. Ignoring ethical issues associated with building and using computerized decision support is **not an option**.

Summary

The path to digital transformation is not an easy or even a straight one. More wide-spread adoption of analytics is a key element of digital transformation for an organization. This chapter considered analytics and decision support paying particular attention to the increasing need for high-velocity decision making. Many tools including BI, analytics, and decision support and other tools and technologies can be used to support the development of an ethical, data-based approach to organizational decision making.

Amazon's Jeff Bezos has pursued the development of a data-based, high-velocity decision making approach using analytics and decision support to improve decision-making outcomes. He warns the key challenge for decision makers is 'one-size-fits-all' decision making. Bezos' approach advocates rapid decision making with less than complete information, where the decision makers use their judgment to react quickly in situations where a decision is reversible.

While this approach has seemingly worked well for Bezos, it is important to consider the role of ethics in making decisions in high-velocity environments. Perhaps there is an opportunity to build questions, such as those proposed by Chessell (2014) into the decision process. Ethical decision making is important for data-driven, data-based, and data-informed decision making. Further consideration must be given to the challenges of ethical decision making in this data-intensive era of digital upheaval and transformation.

Type 1, consequential and irreversible decisions, requires ethical, data-informed decision making, including use of analytics and decision support. Ethical considerations are also very important in making high-velocity, reversible Type 2 decisions. Considering ethical issues is relevant when managers use data-based decision making or implement an algorithmic data-driven decision automation solution. Even though some decisions can be "reversed," some harms cannot be undone and consequences associated with an unethical decision cannot be reversed.

Chapter 5 provides additional actionable advice to managers who are implementing a digital transformation vision and strategy.

CHAPTER 5

Implementing Digital Transformation

Both a digital vision and implementing organization-wide actions are important to digital transformation. Data-based decisions must also be made about practical aspects of implementing digital technologies. This chapter explores the how and what of implementing specific technologies in specific processes in an organization. In general, once the vision is defined then technology shortfalls need to be determined. Investing in technology that is not used or that is difficult to use is a problem to avoid. To encourage agile development and rapid customized implementations it is important to consider focusing initially on small-scale cloud-based solutions. Buying large-scale, packaged solutions is fine for infrastructure changes like a new database environment, but such solutions are rarely transforming.

Selecting appropriate technology is important to implementing a digital vision, but the transformation of processes is also an important implementation concern. Everyone needs to be part of the task of transforming work systems and processes not just IT staff. It is important to broaden the availability of skills needed for implementing a digital transformation vision across functions. Technology is an enabler, people and processes must change to implement a new digital vision.

Also, agile processes[1] are important when implementing a digital transformation strategy. Plans must adjust quickly during implementation to meet changing requirements. Establishing and encouraging a data-centric organization culture must be an early goal as part of implementing new processes and technologies. Promoting data-based decision making also helps during implementation. Finally, implementation fails if customer

---

[1] http://agilemanifesto.org/

needs did not inform the digital vision. Successful digital transformation implementation requires constant collaboration with current and potential customers. In general, a digitally transformed business model values meeting customer needs. Remember successful implementation of new technologies for digital transformation requires commitment of all major stakeholders. Keep stakeholders informed.

Digital transformation involves significant changes that result from applying digital technology in new ways in an organization. For some managers, the notion of digital transformation may be difficult and complex to document, explain, and communicate. This chapter suggests a number of ways to assess and increase the digital maturity of an organization. Complex technology innovations such as the Internet of Things (IoT), cloud computing and storage, radio frequency identifiers (RFID), blockchain, robotics, and mobile computing and telecommunications devices are often an integral part of an organization's digital transformation strategy. Opportunities for artificial intelligence (AI) and machine learning (ML) in decision making are also often explored. Technologies for data collection, storage, management, transfer, and analysis are at the center of digital disruption. The following sections examine: (1) the distinctive features of digital transformation, (2) the role of data in digital transformation, (3) fundamentals of data visualization, (4) understanding data storytelling, and (5) using algorithms to turn data into actions.

Distinctive Features of Digital Transformation

Digital transformation looks different for every business. For some the primary focus is about finding new ways to leverage technological innovation, others identify customer engagement as a top priority for their digital transformation strategy, and some businesses focus on changing an existing business model. For a business, digital transformation may mean pursuing some or perhaps all of these activities. Given the operational, tactical, and strategic nature of digital transformation, one thing is clear: digital transformation equals business transformation (Edmead 2016). The breadth and depth of people, processes, and technology involved in an organization's digital transformation strategy is significant. If we characterize digital transformation as a continuous improvement strategy, it is clear that some organizations and certain industry sectors are further along the journey than others. As the digital landscape continues to evolve, new business models and technological shifts in areas such as AI, ML, and IoT continue to drive organizational change and evolution.

A number of authors have examined digital transformation maturity. Solis (2016) identified six distinct stages of digital transformation maturity: (1) business as usual, (2) test and learn, (3) systemize and strategize, (4) adapt or die, (5) transformed and transforming, and (6) innovate or die. His report advocates "six key elements within the organization that must undergo simultaneous transformation, Analytics, Customer Experience, Governance and Leadership, People and Operations, Technology Integration, and Digital Literacy." Managers should assess where the organization is in terms of these stages. Ideally managers are moving the organization strategically toward stage 6 where a culture of innovation dominates managerial thinking.

Evans (2015) identified six steps that can result in digital transformation maturity. The steps are sequential and are likely to be repeated again and again. **Step 1**: identify your transformation objectives. **Step 2**: study technology enablers in the market. **Step 3**: envision the future platform for digital business. **Step 4**: master the digital services lifecycle. **Step 5**: organize for digital business innovation. **Step 6**: execute an agile journey to the future platform. *Do and Repeat.*

Many vendors of technology products have suggested digital transformation steps, phases, life cycles or approaches. Kolander (2017), product marketing manager at Laserfiche, noted "The concept of the digital workplace has been around for some time, and the definition continues to evolve with new and improved technologies." He suggests five basic steps are: (1) Digitize everything, (2) Organize data and use data in processes, (3) Automate data collection and data processing, (4) Streamline business processes—remove the waste, and (5) Transform the business, drive innovation by leveraging analytics to align processes with business goals.

Digitizing everything is impractical, managers must have a realistic vision for the transformed enterprise. Managers must have some idea about needed changes in the current business model and processes that must change to support the new business model. The real benefit of digital transformation comes from using digital data to help make better decisions.

Digital transformation involves directed technological change. There are however a number of macroeconomic biases associated with technological change. First, there is a capital-bias associated with technology change. Implementing digital technologies and re-engineering processes is capital intensive and managers may want to avoid the capital expenditures. Second, digital transformation is generally labor-augmenting. People can do better work and more of it and that may reduce work force size and increase turnover. Third, a price effect has encouraged skill-biased technological change, and the skill bias seems to be accelerating. Digital transformation is creating a shift in production technology that favors hiring skilled over unskilled labor. These three macroeconomic biases (Acemoglu 2002) can influence digital transformation decisions by managers.

Box 5.1 is an assessment tool for managers to use to evaluate progress on the "digital transformation journey." The questions raise general issues that are worth thinking about and answering.

Box 5.1 *Digital transformation assessment tool (modified from Laserfiche)*

Digital Transformation Assessment Tool

1. Do you have a digital data strategy?
2. Do you have a disaster recovery plan for your data and information?
3. Can your employees easily retrieve data and documents from a digital repository?
4. Do you have a secure and centralized digital content repository?
5. Have you automated your business processes to minimize time-consuming and manual steps?
6. Have you integrated your data and process systems?
7. Can managers monitor IT operations and ensure that IT implementations are aligned with business goals?
8. Does a sound data governance plan ensure security and quality of data?
9. Do you have a strategic vision for how to effectively use data resources, better meet customer needs, and maximize employee performance?

10. Can you analyze past data, especially to predict future outcomes?

11. Are content and data management and process automation strategies aligned with organizational goals?

12. Is your organization an industry leader in implementing innovative and technologically advanced process solutions?

So how do you assess the current stage of digital transformation for an organization? The more questions in Box 5.1 where the answer is **YES**, the further along the organization is in reaching digital transformation maturity. For any gaps, plan for additional steps to reach transformation goals. Ideally an organization will reach the point where a culture of innovation dominates managerial thinking. Implementing a digital transformation vision is an ongoing process of change, a journey. Bilefield (2016) advocates "Building a culture of constant change."

Role of Data in Digital Transformation

Digital transformation is about more than data. The IoT, cloud computing, and mobile devices are technological innovations that are important to digital transformation in many industries. These innovations support individuals, businesses, health care organizations, and governments in collecting, storing, managing, and disseminating data.

In his Forbes article, Newman (2017) ranks IoT as the top trend for digital transformation in 2018. As Newman points out it is not the "Things" that are interesting, it is the data being managed by the many devices that continues to create new opportunities for business.

Newman's (2017) expectations about opportunities and challenges for the growing Internet of Things (IoT) network are many and include:

1. Security is an increasing concern and challenge. The Internet environment has minimal regulation and as IoT continues to grow protecting the privacy and security of data is important.

2. IoT will increasingly drive customer engagement and focused marketing strategies.

3. Expanding opportunities for IoT and data analytics.

The exponential rate at which data is generated is a challenge for organizations. To meaningfully compete, where the focus is on data as a valuable asset, digitally transformative organizations must investigate ways to develop new capabilities to support continuous business process improvement and technology development. To achieve this goal, organizations need to embrace cloud strategies. Organizations need to move away from a siloed system of record to using cloud technologies that will allow them to run applications from anywhere delivering data to end users (Dubash 2017). Using data requires integrated, enterprise-wide data storage solutions.

Cloud computing and IoT promise to tackle complex organizational data challenges. The IoT allows us to generate and collect large volumes of data anytime from anywhere using a variety of mobile, sensor, and other devices. Cloud computing provides a path to direct that data to the right place for storage, processing, and analysis. The cloud can help connect IoT devices and provide storage capabilities as well as support new applications for analytics. While the two technologies are different, innovation in the cloud and for IoT will create new opportunities for both technologies.

Digital transformation means using data, visualizing relationships, data enabling processes, assisting in understanding customers, and making better and faster decisions. Let's examine data visualization.

Fundamentals of Data Visualization

Visualizing data means that we can see relationships that exist in a related set of data. A visualization is often a short cut for understanding an underlying pattern in data. The danger is that the pattern is spurious and that we fail to test for the significance of the relationship. So what are "best practices" for visualizing a data set? Should we start with descriptive information on the data set? Should we have a prior hypothesis that guides our analysis? Should we try a number of techniques and tools and see if we find a relationship?

The answers to these questions are complex and managers should be cautious about the the technical arguments some experts might make. In general, best practices are conservative. We seek to ensure that a relationship really exists in the data set and that it is meaningful and useful to its intended user. Be cautious in data analysis and display and use a supposition or hypothesis to guide a limited number of statistical tests for significant relationships. A hypothesis is a tentative explanation that can be tested. The dangers of undirected or unplanned data analysis are real and it is easy for analysts to fall into the trap of testing so many relationships that by chance they find a spurious or false relationship.

In data-based decision making, it is desirable to begin with a hypothesis about a relationship and then find a data set that will allow us to test the relationship. The data set needs to be sufficiently large or meaningful and derived in a manner that does not have bias. The relationship must be from the data and not an artifact of how the data was gathered. A data analyst should begin with a descriptive analysis of a relevant data set. Then test a limited number of hypotheses to reduce the chances we will find a false or chance relationship. The scientific approach provides safe guards to insure the repeatability of the results and the truthfulness that we should demand.

Data visualization can convey incorrect information as well as show meaningful relationships. It is important that everyone associated with creating and interpreting a visualization uses caution in choosing the visualization tools and in interpreting the results. Visualization should tell an accurate story. The presence of a powerful visualization can actually hinder our data-based decision making if we are misled to think that something is true when in fact it is false.

We begin a data-based decision making process with a question we want to ask and a hypothesized answer. For example, we want to know: Who are our best customers? We think that married women with children are our best customers. The preliminary statement helps define data we need to analyze to verify a relationship. So we need to obtain purchase and demographic data and then find tools that will let us test the relationship. The visualization alone is not enough, we must use statistical tests to ensure that the relationship shown in the visualization is meaningful. We need to correct for the bias that would lead us to incorrectly conclude that a relationship exists when in fact it does not exist. We don't want a false positive—a type I error—anymore that we want a type II error—a false negative.

According to Vitaly Friedman (2008), the "main goal of data visualization is to communicate information clearly and effectively through graphical means." Data analysis insures we are effectively examining the data. We study and summarize data with the intent to find useful information and develop conclusions. We need effective data analysis and not just effective data visualization. Showing a false relationship is not helpful.

Edward Tufte (1983; 2001) wrote a classic on advanced data visualization. He cautions against decorative and noninformative content added to charts. He notes one can deceive with visualizations by picking deceptive scales or selecting data. To avoid distortions, Tufte argues for using all the relevant data and presenting it accurately and in a visually attractive manner.

Further, Ryan Bell (2012) suggests developing visualizations using the following steps: (1) understand the problem domain, (2) get sound data, (3) show the data and show comparisons; (4) incorporate visual design principles; (5) allow for quick visual comparisons; (6) add extra levels of information and preserve the high-level summary data; (7) add axes or coding patterns; and (8) add a network metaphor to show complex connections. The basic visualization design principles are: (1) align and position elements, (2) create clear contrasts and a visual hierarchy, (3) create visual unity with repetition of design elements across representations, and (4) use proximity and grouping of design elements with white space (cf. Tchakirides 2011).

As Bell notes "Business analysts, IT staff and knowledge workers will need more skills designing, building and using fluid, interactive, dynamic visualizations." A good starting point is the theory and practice writings of Edward Tufte (www.edwardtufte.com). Finding and sharing meaning is our goal. Better visualization tools increase our ability to understand and persuade.

Understanding Data Storytelling

Managers must understand the fundamentals of data analysis and data visualization, including some tools and techniques, for effective data-based decision making. In this era of digital disruption we need to go further than visualization and provide managers with the skills to use data to communicate their ideas. Data storytelling goes beyond data visualization. With data storytelling managers use data to communicate a message.

Morgan (2016) suggests that data visualization is the proof or evidence that may be used to answer the "what" question, while data storytelling is the context that may be leveraged to answer the "why" question.

In the world of digital transformation, many of our stories may be characterized as "data stories." According to Brown (2018), "Real data storytelling is a way to share facts in the form that your listener understands, appreciates and remembers best—the story." Data storytelling means developing a compelling narrative that provides people with hooks to access the plot and main characters. Like all good stories, data stories should have a beginning, middle, and end. These stories allow us to use engaging narratives together with data anchors to communicate a finely tuned persuasive story. Data stories may be used to sell ideas to key decision makers about many topics including new technologies, potential markets, and new products and services.

With increasing data volume and data complexity it is often difficult to see the forest from the trees. We must identify and craft a focused data story using the most effective analytics. Knowing the audience is essential when developing an effective data story, there is no one-size-fits all approach (Morgan 2016). In her article, Brown (2018) articulates this succinctly "make your data stories real stories, and align data storytelling with the desires and communication style of your audience." As illustrated in Figure 5.1, effective data storytelling is a culmination of analysis and thought about the audience, the narrative and the visualization.

Data visualization and data storytelling are means to improve decision making. Part of implementing a digital transformation vision and strategy

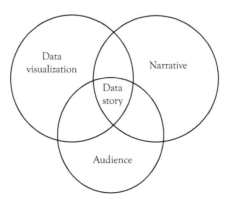

Figure 5.1 Data storytelling approach

is improving the way data is used in decision making, which means increased data visualization and more effective data storytelling. Kumar (2017) offers a step-by-step approach for creating effective data stories:

1. Plan your story, assess a couple of alternatives before selecting a strategic approach.
2. Identify the main focus of your story—what are you trying to achieve?
3. Use powerful headings in your story.
4. Develop a road-map—articulate all of the key points you want the audience to know about the story, a chart or an analysis. Stick to the rule of three, group your ideas until you are left with three main ideas. Add facts, analogies, and examples to the three main ideas.
5. Keep the conclusion brief—emphasize the highlights. Ask what lasting impression do you wish to leave with the audience? What's the call to action?

Morgan's (2016) views align with those of Kumar, she emphasizes the need for a focused data story. Morgan advocates the importance of staying focused and avoiding distractions around the analysis process or the operational details of the project. Figure 5.2 illustrates a process for developing a data story. Start with asking questions about the data, then the audience, develop a simple message and finally tell a story.

Almost 10 years ago, Google's Chief Economist Hal Varian commented "the ability to take data—to be able to understand it, to process it, to extract value from it, to visualize it, to communicate it—that's going to be a hugely important skill in the next decades" (McKinsey 2009). We now need to identify and develop the key skills required to analyze data for successful data storytelling to support and enable improved data-based decision making in organizations.

Using Algorithms to Turn Data into Actions

While the concepts associated with Artificial Intelligence (AI) and Machine Learning (ML) are not new, the pace at which these technological innovations are evolving continues at significant speed. Many vendors, consultants, and researchers who previously focused on "app"

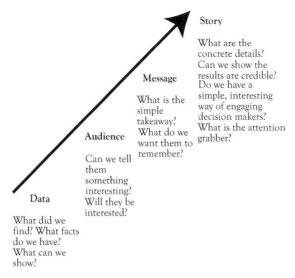

Story

What are the concrete details? Can we show the results are credible? Do we have a simple, interesting way of engaging decision makers? What is the attention grabber?

Message

What is the simple takeaway? What do we want them to remember?

Audience

Can we tell them something interesting? Will they be interested?

Data

What did we find? What facts do we have? What can we show?

Figure 5.2 Creating a data story

development focus on algorithm development for distribution and resale. In 2016, Gartner coined the term "Algorithm Economy" (van der Meulen 2016).

Gartner describes this phenomenon as disruptive and innovative. An opportunity for software developers to refocus their "app" endeavours and instead engage with the idea of an algorithm marketplace. The idea of an algorithm marketplace is that innovators can build "algorithms and other software components to be brokered. These algorithms are not stand-alone apps, but are meant to be used as building blocks within tailored solutions."

Both algorithms and AI are attracting considerable attention. In a recent Gartner paper, Panetta (2017) indicates that AI is at the top of its hype curve. There are many competing definitions for Artificial Intelligence. According to one Deloitte report, van Duin and Bakhski (2017) state AI "is concerned with getting computers to do tasks that would normally require human intelligence." Artificial Intelligence is not discipline-specific, it leverages theories, practices, and existing knowledge from a variety of areas including computer science, psychology, decision sciences, information systems, linguistics, philosophy, and others.

Managers in organizations large and small are trying to come to grips with the prospect of AI in general and the possibilities within the context of their organizations. Data-based decision making can help managers assess the possibilities. Potentially AI, ML and cognitive technologies can assist with data-based decision making. For example, cognitive technologies like neural network and natural language processing (NLP) are being used to make business processes and products smarter. In Allen's (2018) article, innovator Elon Musk commented "competition for AI superiority at (the) national level (is the) most likely cause of WW3." AI is potentially transformative.

Machine Learning (ML) is an important subdiscipline of AI, "that provides computers with the ability to learn without being explicitly programmed. ML focuses on the development of computer programs that can change when exposed to new data" (Marr 2016). Marr identifies diverse use cases for AI including:

1. Financial trading, including predicting changes and executing trades at high speeds and high volume;
2. Health care practice, for example reviewing mammography scans;
3. Marketing personalization, such as direct mail and targeted ads;
4. Fraud detection including distinguishing between legitimate and fraudulent transactions among buyers and sellers;
5. Making recommendations by analyzing your activity and comparing it to millions of other users;
6. NLP where digital avatars chat and stand in for customer service agents.

Possibilities for smart technologies are vast and continue to change, evolve, and mature at a significant pace. Jeff Bezos at Amazon discussed AI and ML. He explained

> much of what we do with ML happens beneath the surface. ML drives our algorithms for demand forecasting, product search ranking, product and deal recommendations, merchandising placements, fraud detection, translations, and much more. Though less visible, much of the impact of ML will be of this type–quietly but meaningfully improving core operations.[2]

---

[2] Bezos "Obsessive Customer Focus" Key to Winning. https://amazon.com/p/feature/z6o9g6sysxur57t

As organizations identify new opportunities for AI the demand for highly skilled practitioners in this area grows. In her recent Forbes article "Winning the War for AI Talent," Shein (2018) identifies the need for organizations to attract the right talent "data scientists, robotics and AI engineers, and workers with experience in deep neural networks, big data and analytics" as well as other technical areas. Perhaps some of these technical areas do not even exist yet. Further Jeremy Barnes, Chief Architect at Element AI 9 (Madhavan 2018) advocates for the need to hire individuals who have both technical and domain knowledge. He maintains that a deep knowledge of the business, its processes, and domain-specific knowledge coupled with technical expertise is fundamental to AI success.

Building a talent pool is one key pillar of an organization's digital transformation strategy, but especially for an AI focused vision. Once some talent is available to help with assessing possibilities during data-based decision making, the next step is to identify possible business problems that could be solved using AI technologies like ML. It is essential that these transformational possibilities are identified, explored, and prioritized in relation to strategic importance.

Once the first transformation project has been identified and approved, the action loop in Figure 5.3 is a useful guide to ensure that the project stays aligned with and focused on the business problem.

Step 1 is to identify a business problem that you want to solve. This might be an area of high organizational importance and/or the data set is high quality.

Step 2 is to build a simple solution for your problem. This involves examining the data set, processing the data into a format that is accessible for ML, training the model, generating the result and evaluating its performance (Forbes 2017). Once the model has been trained and several iterations are complete to refine the variables and to develop confidence in the results, you can move to step three.

Step 3 is to use the results to operationalize business action.

AI experts recommend that implementing algorithms to take business action should be small-scale at the outset to assist with process augmentation over automation (Madhavan 2018). Proposed AI capabilities should be assessed during data-based decision making to determine how they achieve business goals rather than salary savings (Madhavan 2018; Shein 2018).

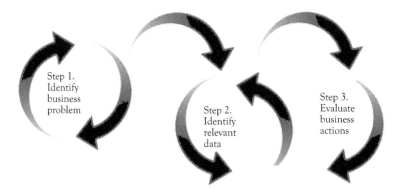

Figure 5.3 Business problem—business action loop

Summary

Digital transformation will look different for every business. This chapter examined digital transformation maturity. Also, it emphasized two fundamental tools of data-based decision making. First, data visualization is defined and various approaches to effective data visualization are reviewed. Visualizing data means that we can see relationships in the data if they exist. Data-based decision making helps to insure we effectively examine the data. We need effective data analysis and not just effective data visualization. Edward Tufte (1983; 2001) wrote a classic on advanced data visualization that can guide us. Second, in a world evolving from digital transformation, many of our decision analyses can be characterized as "data stories." Data visualization and data storytelling are means to improve data-based decision making. Part of implementing a digital transformation strategy is successfully improving the way data is used in decision making—that means increased data visualization and more effective data storytelling. Finally, AI tools like machine learning algorithms can be key elements in using data as part of a digital transformation strategy. To gain benefits, it is particularly important to tackle important organizational business problems through focused actions that leverage organizational talent and data to drive more efficient and effective business models.

CHAPTER 6

Finding a Way Forward

Digital disruption is changing how organizations create value and deliver goods and services. Digital disruption is transforming industries. The disruption manifests itself in new digital tools, digital services, and expanded data capture and analysis. Digital transformation initiatives by managers in one firm in an industry promote more rapid and ongoing innovation in that industry and in others. Successful adoption of new approaches using digital tools and data leads to more change and more disruption. We have a digital device society, with smart phones and IoT common place. Digital disruption is not an "if it happens," but rather a "when it happens" phenomenon. Digital disruption is the change that occurs when new digital technologies and business models affect the value proposition of existing goods and services. Understanding and acting appropriately when digital disruptions occur is necessary. Managers should embrace change and build upon innovation.

Analyzing data are now a core decision support task for many organizations. Managers must try to derive greater value from multiple, diverse data sources using analytical tools and decision support applications. Digitalization of activities and processes has led to an explosive growth in data. Big Data has hence increased the need for analytics. This major change has increased the need for managers to understand the possibilities of these technologies and their application in a variety of areas including financial services, manufacturing, retail, pharmaceuticals, health care, and government. As managers across these sectors formulate IS/IT strategies and make investments, it is essential for them to consider how data-based decision making and analytics can contribute to improved decision making, improved information and knowledge management, and ultimately to greater organizational success.

Most decisions are what Jeff Bezos labeled as Type 2 decisions that can be reversed, altered, and changed. The cost of remedying a suboptimal

Type 2 decision varies, but use the data you have, analyze it, develop a data story, share the story and get feedback, then go for it. Commit and implement. Many of these operational and tactical decisions should be a priority for implementing advanced analytics and algorithms. When a decision is made again and again we need to find ways to make the decision better and faster.

Strategic, Type 1 decisions deserve and require more thoughtful data-based and data-informed decision making. New data may need to be collected and analyzed. Implementation and commitment may need to be made in stages. Knowing that a decision once made and implemented cannot be reversed is a daunting thought. There is no going back. The decision to digitally transform an organization is a Type 1 decision. Craft a vision for digital transformation and analyze it carefully, then senior managers must decide and make a commitment to the vision. Middle-level managers will and should be responsible for the related Type 1 and Type 2 decisions that must be made to realize the digital vision in that specific organization. Developing a clearly stated vision statement and writing a scenario describing the transformed organization will help guide subsequent data-based decision making.

Many busy managers want to grasp the basics of analytics, data-based decision making, and digital transformation. That quest has begun. Prior chapters discussed decision making and digital transformation, data-based decision making, analytics and high-velocity decision making, and finally implementing digital transformation. The overall goal for prior chapters has been to help managers become more knowledgeable about the what, how, and why of data-based decision making. One hopes greater awareness of the importance of data-based decision making will help managers better assess, choose, and successfully implement digital transformation competitive opportunities.

Figure 6.1 depicts the factors that are determining the winners and losers in the race to implement digital transformation visions and strategies. The basic relationships in the model identify data-based decision making as the key independent factor that can alter outcomes and results in organizations including successful implementation of a digital transformation vision. The relationship is moderated primarily by alignment of organizational elements, adequate and appropriate resources, a skilled

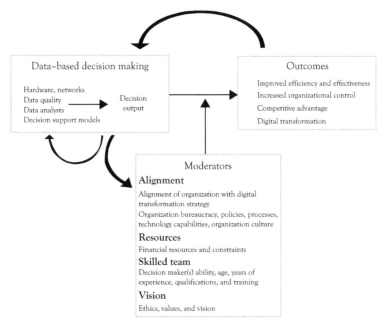

Figure 6.1 Factors that influence organization outcomes

team, and the digital transformation vision itself. Characteristics of individual decision makers and organizational factors are especially important to success.

Digital transformation involves making decisions about technology trade-offs and ideally choices are data-informed and fact-based. Data-based decision making is both a process and a culture. Some managers and organizations already value using data and facts to make decisions. Part of digital transformation is to make systematic use of data in decision making. Decision making using data and facts is both a precursor to digital transformation and the reinforcement of a data culture and improved data-based decision making is and should be a necessary consequence of digital transformation.

Global business activity is accelerating and decision-making activities and processes must be responsive to changing business needs and a high-velocity decision environment. Understanding what is occurring can increase the adaptive response of managers.

Finally, understanding the need for new technology supported processes, better use of data in decision making, and possibilities for revised and innovative business models is not sufficient. Managers must understand how to successfully implement digital transformation competitive opportunities. A strategy without an implementation plan and action taking is wishful thinking.

Society is in the midst of profound and irreversible change. Data are everywhere and data provide the opportunity for new business models, increased efficiencies, and greater effectiveness in meeting customer needs. The digital world is volatile, uncertain, complex, and ambiguous. We cope with digital disruption by developing a vision, understanding technology opportunities, simplifying our processes, and using data, and by clarifying our intent and purpose.[1]

What can we conclude about the broad questions we identified in the introduction? First, we asked how can managers become data-based decision makers? Second, we asked how can digital transformation become part of an organizational strategy? Third, we sought to identify the new skills managers must develop to implement digital transformation? Finally, we asked how will we know an organization has been successfully transformed? So what have we concluded?

First, managers can become data-based decision makers by accepting and understanding that many, if not most, decisions should be based on and informed by data. Asking the "right" questions and getting factual answers is the starting point to becoming a more systematic decision maker who uses relevant data sources and prepares appropriate analyses. Analyses don't need to be complex, rather tools like data visualization can help identify meaningful relationships for follow-up analysis.

Second, digital transformation can become part of an organizational strategy when managers at all levels learn about leading edge technologies and explore opportunities. It is important to pilot process improvement projects, create analytics and decision support for customer facing staff, and encourage risk taking and innovation. Managers need to take measured risks. Successful change needs to be rewarded quickly and showcased. Failed innovation must be ended quickly, but those involved must be encouraged to try again. Opportunistic decision making based

---

[1] Bob Johansen http://iftf.org/bobjohansen

on data must be encouraged as part of the digital transformation journey. The path to digital maturity is neither short nor easy, the path often involves a steep learning curve, some waste, and false starts. Embarking on a digital transformation journey must start with experimentation and innovation. Data must be captured and analyzed to determine what worked and what aspects of the change need revision or even elimination. A digital transformation vision and strategy should have broad scope and ambitious objectives. Digitally immature organizations need to have decision makers who focus broadly on technology and have strategies that are not only operational in focus.

Third, the new skills managers must develop include analyzing data, visualizing data and data storytelling. Every manager does not need to be a data scientist, rather every manager should strive to be an intelligent consumer of data and an expert at analyzing and using data. A good manager is a good data storyteller.

Finally, we will know an organization has been successfully transformed when a data-centric culture is entrenched, when data-based decision making is rewarded, when the organization is reporting strong performance and results over a few years, and when performance exceeds that of organizations serving the same or similar needs. We want to create a self-reinforcing cycle of ongoing digital transformation where successful change leads to further success.

Agility is the way forward to find a successful digital transformation. Following a plan for digital transformation is important, but adapting the plan quickly to changing requirements and needs is more important.[2] Enjoy the digital journey!

---

[2] http://agilemanifesto.org/

Glossary

Algorithm economy—algorithms enable computing machines to make sense of data and use it. Developing them for purposes of distribution and resale is a recent activity. Companies are monetizing these algorithms to realize their economic value.

Analytics—"extensive use of data, statistical and quantitative analysis, exploratory and predictive models, and fact-based management to drive decisions and actions. The analytics may be input for human decisions or drive fully automated decisions" (Davenport and Harris 2007, p. 7). Analytics refers to quantitative and statistical analysis and manipulation of data to derive meaning. Analytics is a broad umbrella term that includes business analytics and data analytics.

Big data—very large data volumes that are complex and varied, and often collected and must be analyzed in real time.

Business analytics—use of data and quantitative and qualitative tools and techniques to improve operations and to support business decision making. Emphasis on using statistical and management science techniques, including data mining, to develop predictive and prescriptive models.

Business intelligence—umbrella term that describe a set of concepts and methods to improve business decision making by using fact-based decision support systems. Also, refers to a category of software tools that can be used to extract and analyze data from corporate databases.

Cloud analytics—a data analytics service provided through a public or private cloud.

Customer engagement—establishing a strong business relationship between a customer and an organization. Customer engagement may be a strategic objective of an organization's digital transformation strategy.

Data—relevant facts, figures, and digital content captured in information systems. Raw data are the bits and bytes stored electronically.

Data analytics—applying quantitative and statistical methods to analyze large, complex data sets. See analytics and business analytics.

Data-based decision making—a broad concept that prescribes an ongoing process of collecting and analyzing different types of data to aid in making fact-based, routine and nonroutine decisions. Use of diverse data types from a variety of sources. A process where quantitative data is balanced with "softer" data that is more descriptive in nature.

Data-centric culture—data is highly valued in the organization. The importance of data is embedded in everything we do.

Data-centric organization—an organization with policies and a culture that encourage and reward the use of data in products, processes, and decision making. Also, sometimes called a data-driven or data-informed organization.

Data-driven decision making—collection and analysis of data to make decisions. Data "drives" the decision making and decisions are made using data or facts rather than intuition. Data-driven decision making is often used interchangeably with the term data-based decision making, but it often implies decision automation using artificial intelligence and algorithms.

Data governance—processes and procedures implemented by organizations to ensure data quality.

Data-informed decision making—term used when data and facts are an influential factor in decision making, but not the only factor.

Data storytelling—using a combination of data facts and a qualitative "story" that provides effective communication of a business message.

Data visualization—communication of data using visual prompts or representations such as charts, graphs, and other illustrations.

Decision support system (DSS)—a computer-based information system that supports individual or team decision making. Five primary types: communications-driven, data-driven, document-driven, knowledge-driven, and data-driven DSS.

Digital transformation—use of new information technologies such as analytics, mobile devices, social media and smart embedded devices to change and improve business processes, improve performance, alter business models, enhance products, and change customer experiences. Integration of digital technologies into all areas of an organization, fundamentally changing operations.

Digital transformation maturity—amount of progress in implementing actions reimaging or reinventing an organization, typically leveraging existing and new digital technology.

Digitalization—enabling, improving, and/or changing business operations and business processes and activities using digital data and technologies. Often used interchangeably with digitization and digital transformation.

Digitization—using digital data to automate business processes and workflows.

Ethical decision making—application of moral rules, codes, or principles to guide choices for right and truthful behavior. A process of evaluating and choosing among alternatives in a manner consistent with ethical principles. Generally part of data-based decision-making processes.

Fact—a statement or numerical value consistent with reality or that can be proven with evidence. A fact is something known to have happened or to exist. In general, a fact can be verified as true.

High velocity decision making—use of streamlined, rapid decision processes focused on issues while ensuring decision making processes are thoughtful and goal-oriented.

Internet of Things (IoT)—computing or "smart" devices often with sensor capability and the ability to collect, share, and transfer data using the Internet.

Machine Learning (ML)—a subset of AI systems that use algorithms to learn from data and improve based on experience without being explicitly reprogrammed.

Operating or function-specific decisions—day-to-day, routine decisions with a concise decision question and a clear, well-defined, and structured algorithm to make a choice among alternatives.

Predictive analytics—general term for using simple and complex models to support anticipatory decision making. Often a process of using a quantitative model and current real-time or historical data to generate a score that is predictive of future behavior.

Prescriptive analytics—manipulate large data sets to make recommendations. Decision support that prescribes or recommends an action, rather than a forecast or a summary report.

Rationality—consistent with or based on logic and facts. Behavior that demonstrates good sense and sound judgment.

Reporting analytics—Descriptive or reporting analytics describes or summarizes past results, actions, or activities.

Strategic decisions—complex, nonroutine, unstructured decisions involving many different and connected parts. Some variables may not be well understood, often information required to make the decision may be unavailable, incomplete, and in some situations information may be known to be flawed or inaccurate. These decisions usually involve a high degree of uncertainty about outcomes. If implemented, strategic decisions often result in major changes in an organization.

Tactical decisions—broader decision questions than operational decisions, semistructured in nature, some but not all information necessary to make the decision is available, primarily internally focused and made by middle-level managers.

Bibliography

Acemoglu, D. 2002. "Directed Technical Change," *Review of Economic Studies* 69 (4, 241, Oct), pp. 781–809.

Agile 2018. "Manifesto for Agile Software Development" February 14, 2018 from URL http://agilemanifesto.org/

Ahmad, Y. 2016. "Teradata—5 Benefits to Data Analytics." Retrieved on October 11, 2017 from URL http://blogs.teradata.com/data-points/5-big-benefits-data-analytics-positive-business-outcomes/

Allen, G.C. 2018. "Putin and Musk are Right: Whoever Masters AI Will Run the World." February 14, 2018 from URL https://edition.cnn.com/2017/09/05/opinions/russia-weaponize-ai-opinion-allen/index.html

Asadi, S., C.F. Breidbach, M.J. Davern, and G. Shanks. 2016. "Ethical Implications of Big Data Analytics." *Research-in-Progress Papers*, 24. https://aisel.aisnet.org/ecis2016_rip/24

Astley, W.G., R. Axelson, R.J. Butler, D.J. Hickson, and D.C. Wilson. 1981. *An Arena Theory of Organizational Decision Processes*, Unpublished Manuscript, University of Bradford.

Barney, J. 1991. "Firm Resources and Sustained Competitive Advantage." *Journal of Management* 17, no. 1, pp. 99–120.

Bell, R. 2012. "Eight Principles of Data Visualization," *Information Management*, August 17, 2017 from URL http://information-management.com/news/Eight-Principles-of-Data-Visualization-10023032-1.html?ET=information mgmt:e3469:2078848a:&st=email&utm_source=editorial&utm_medium=email&utm_campaign=IM_Da

Bezos , J. 2017. "One Why it is always day One at Amazon", October 26, 2017 from URL https://amazon.com/p/feature/z6o9g6sysxur57t

BI Survey 16. 2017. "Top Business Intelligence Trends 2017: What 2,800 BI Professionals Really Think," Retrieved from March 20, 2017 from URL http://bi-survey.com/top-business-intelligence-trends-2017

Bourgeois, III, L.J., and K.M. Eisenhardt. 1988. "Strategic Decision Processes in High Velocity Environments: Four Cases in the Microcomputer Industry." *Management Science*, pp. 816–35, July 1, 2017 from URL http://pubsonline.informs.org/doi/abs/10.1287/mnsc.34.7.816

Brown, M.S. 2018. "He Turned Data Storytelling Success into Data Storytelling Failure. Here's What Went Wrong." February 2, 2017 from URL. https://forbes.com/sites/metabrown/2018/01/30/he-turned-data-storytelling-success-into-data-storytelling-failure-heres-what-went-wrong/#51c7894e48a5

Capgemini Consulting 2011. "Digital Transformation: A Roadmap for Billion-Dollar Organizations." August 21, 2017 From URL https://Capgemini. Com/Resource-File-Access/Resource/Pdf/Digital_Transformation__A_ Road-Map_For_Billion-Dollar_Organizations.Pdf

Chen, H., R. Chiang, and V. Storey. 2012. "Business Intelligence and Analytics: From Big Data to Big Impact." *MIS Quarterly* 36, no. 4, pp. 1165–88. Retrieved from http://jstor.org/stable/41703503

Chessell, M. 2014. "Ethics for Big Data and Analytics." July 23, 2017 from URL http://ibmbigdatahub.com/sites/default/files/whitepapers_reports_file/ TCG%20Study%20Report%20-%20Ethics%20for%20BD%26A.pdf

Choudhuri, S. 2017. "The Data Differentiator: How Data Is Driving Digital Transformation." February 15, 2018 from URL https://liaison.com/ blog/2017/10/16/data-differentiator-data-driving-digital-transformation/

Court, D. September 2012. "Putting Big Data and Advanced Analytics to Work." *McKinsey and Co.* Video feature, January 17, 2018 from URL http:// mckinsey.com/insights/marketing_sales/putting_big_data_and_advanced_ analytics_to_work

Data visualization, from Wikipedia, the free encyclopedia, Janaury 17, 2018 from URL http://en.wikipedia.org/wiki/ Data_visualization

Davenport, T.H. 2009. "How to Design Smart Business Experiments." *Strategic Direction* 25, no. 8.

Davenport, T.H., and J.G. Harris. 2007. *Competing on Analytics: The New Science of Winning*. Harvard Business School Press.

Davenport, T.H., D. Cohen, and A. Jacobson. May 2005. "Competing on Analytics." November 17, 2017 from URL http://babsonknowledge.org/ analytics.pdf

Dimension Data. 2017. "The Digital Workplace Report: Transforming Your Business." August 21, 2017 from URL http://www2.dimensiondata.com/en/ microsites//media/95C5923C59FD4437B870929D3396F891.ashx

Drucker, P. 1992. *Managing for the Future*. Oxford: Butterworth Heinemann.

Dubash, M. 2017. "Digital Transformation in the Cloud: How the Cloud Can Save Your Business from Oblivion." February 5, 2018 from URL http:// zdnet.com/article/digital-transformation-in-the-cloud/

Dykes, B. 2017. "Big Data: Forget Volume and Variety, Focus On Velocity," *Forbes*, June 28, 2017 from URL https://forbes.com/sites/brentdykes/2017/06/28/ big-data-forget-volume-and-variety-focus-on-velocity/#5de2336f7d67

Edmead, M. 2016. "Digital Transformation: Why It's Important to Your Organization, CIO." February 14, 2018 from URL https://cio.com/ article/3063620/it-strategy/digital-transformation-why-its-important-to-your-organization.html

Eisenhardt, K.M. September 1989. "Making Fast Strategic Decisions in High-Velocity Environments." *The Academy of Management Journal* 32, no. 3, pp. 543–76, November 14, 2017 URL https://jstor.org/stable/256434

Eisenhardt, K.M., and M.J. Zbaracki. December 1992. "Strategic Decision Making." *Strategic Management Journal* 13, pp. 17–37. doi:10.1002/smj.4250130904

Ernst and Young 2017. "Why Digital Governance Matter." August 21, 2017 from URL http://ey.com/gl/en/services/advisory/ey-why-digital-governance-matters

Enderle, R. 2013. "Data Analytics Will Fail If Executives Ignore the Numbers." *CIO*, January 4, 2018 from URL http://cio.com/article/2389409/data-management/data-analytics-will-fail-if-executives-ignore-the-numbers.html

Enderle, R. 2014. "Are We Too Stupid to Let Watson Make Us Smarter?" *CIO Online*, February 14, 2018 from URL https://cio.com/article/2378707/big-data/are-we-too-stupid-to-let-watson-make-us-smarter-.html

Evans, N.B. 2015. "6 Steps for Digital Transformation," *CIO*, October 1, 2017 from URL https://cio.com/article/2988012/it-management/6-steps-for-digital-transformation.html

Forbes 2017. "Eight Easy Steps to Get Started Learning Artificial Intelligence." February 2, 2018 from URL https://forbes.com/sites/quora/2017/04/05/eight-easy-steps-to-get-started-learning-artificial-intelligence/#3d7ea5bfb117

Friedman, V. 2008. "Data Visualization and Infographics," *Smashing Magazine*, January 14, 2018 from URL http://smashingmagazine.com/2008/01/14/monday-inspiration-data-visualization-and-infographics/

Frick, W. 2014. "An Introduction to Data-driven Decisions for Managers Who Don't Like Math." *Harvard Business Review.*

Grossman, R. 2016. "The Industries That Are Being Disrupted the Most by Digital." *Harvard Business Review*, March 21, 2018 from URL https://hbr.org/2016/03/the-industries-that-are-being-disrupted-the-most-by-digital

Heavin, C., and D. Power. 2017. "How Do Data Analytics Support Data-based Decision-Making?", November 28, 2017 from URL http://dssresources.com/faq/index.php?action=artikel&id=405

Heavin, C., and D. Power. 2017. "What Are Current Trends in BI and Data Analytics?", September 9, 2017 from URL http://dssresources.com/faq/index.php?action=artikel&id=383

IBM Analytics Quotient (AQ) quiz at URL http://www-01.ibm.com/software/analytics/aq/

IDC 2017. Data Age, October 20, 2017 from URL https://seagate.com/files/www-content/our-story/trends/files/Seagate-WP-DataAge2025-March-2017.pdf.

iScoop 2016. "Digitization, digitalization and digital transformation: the differences". Retrieved May 27, 2016 from URL https://i-scoop.eu/digitization-digitalization-digital-transformation-disruption/

Jeffrey, B. 2016. "Annual Letter to Shareholders." April 6, 2017 from URL https://sec.gov/Archives/edgar/data/1018724/000119312516530910/d168744dex991.htm

Jeffry, B. 2017a. "Annual Letter to Shareholders." April 12, 2017 from URL https://sec.gov/Archives/edgar/data/1018724/000119312517120198/d373368dex991.htm

Jeffry, B. 2017b. "2016 Annual Letter to Shareholders." April 12, 2017 from URL https://amazon.com/p/feature/z6o9g6sysxur57t

Johansen, B. Institute for the Future, February 20, 2018 from URL http://iftf.org/bobjohansen

Jones, S. 2016. "How Data Analytics Can Give You a Competitive Advantage." October 11, 2017 from URL https://birst.com/blog/%E2%80%8Bhow-data-analytics-can-give-you-a-competitive-advantage/

Kane, G., D. Palmer, A.N. Phillips, D. Kiron, and N. Buckley. 2015. "Strategy, Not Technology, Drives Digital Transformation—Becoming a Digitally Mature Enterprise." *MIT Sloan Management Review*, January 13, 2018 from URL https://sloanreview.mit.edu/projects/strategy-drives-digital-transformation/

Kanter, B. 2013. "Why Data Informed VS Data Driven?" *Beth's Blog*, July 23, 2017 from URL http://bethkanter.org/data-informed/

Kerschberg, B. 2017. "How Digital Disrupts Operations." *Business Processes and Customer Experience*, August 27, 2017 from URL https://forbes.com/sites/benkerschberg/2017/03/01/how-digital-disrupts-operations-and-business-processes-as-well-as-customer-experience/#40ba59e25466

Kipling, R. 1902. "I Keep Six Honest Serving Men," *The Elephant's Child*, February 1, 2018 from URL http://kiplingsociety.co.uk/poems_serving.htm

Kolander, C. 2017. "Digital Transformation's Increasingly Important Role," *Q&A at ECM Connection*, Januaray 4, 2018 from URL https://www.ecmconnection.com/doc/digital-transformation-s-increasingly-important-role-0001

Kumar, S. 2017. "The Art of Story Telling in Data Science and How to Create Data Stories?", February 13, 2018 from URL https://analyticsvidhya.com/blog/2017/10/art-story-telling-data-science/

Lebied, M. 2016. "Top 11 Business Intelligence and Analytics Trends for 2017." *Business Intelligence*, December 15, 2017 from URL http://datapine.com/blog/business-intelligence-trends-2017

LEO Computers Society, URL http://leo-computers.org.uk/index.htm

Lewis, P.V. 1985. "Defining 'Business Ethics': Like Nailing Jello to a Wall." *Journal of Business Ethics*, pp. 377–83. doi:10.1007/BF02388590

Madhavan, R. 2018. "Avoiding Common Mistakes in Applying AI to Business Problems—with Jeremy Barnes of Element AI." February 18, 2018 from URL https://techemergence.com/avoiding-common-mistakes-in-b2b-ai-applications/

Mandinach, E.B., E.S. Gummer, and R.D. Muller. 2011. "The Complexities of Integrating Data-Driven Decision Making into Professional Preparation in Schools of Education: It's Harder Than You Think." February 13, 2018 from URL http://educationnorthwest.org/sites/default/files/gummer-mandinach-report-summary.pdf

Marr, B. 2016a. "The Top 10 AI and Machine Learning Use Cases Everyone Should Know About." September 30, 2017 from URL https://forbes.com/sites/bernardmarr/2016/09/30/what-are-the-top-10-use-cases-for-machine-learning-and-ai/#5a4f59cf94c9

Marr, B. 2016b. "The 18 Best Analytics Tools Every Business Manager Should Know." September 10, 2017 from URL https://forbes.com/sites/bernardmarr/2016/02/04/the-18-best-analytics-tools-every-business-manager-should-know/#4a0c101d5d39

Marr, B. 2017. "The Amazing Ways How Artificial Intelligence and Machine Learning Is Used in Healthcare." January 15, 2018 from URL, https://forbes.com/sites/bernardmarr/2017/10/09/the-amazing-ways-how-artificial-intelligence-and-machine-learning-is-used-in-healthcare/2/#2f9c78542db9

Maycotte, H.O. 2015. "Be Data-Informed, Not Data-Driven, For Now." July 21, 2017 from URL https://forbes.com/sites/homaycotte/2015/01/13/data-informed-not-data-driven-for-now/#6cd93b7cf5b7

Mandinach, E.B., E.S. Gummer, and R.D. Muller. 2011. "The Complexities of Integrating Data-Driven Decision Making into Professional Preparation in Schools of Education: It's Harder Than You Think." February 13, 2018 from URL http://educationnorthwest.org/sites/default/files/gummer-mandinach-report-summary.pdf

McAfee, A., and E. Brynjolfsson. 2012. "Big Data: The Management Revolution." *Harvard Business Review*, October.

Moore, K. 2014. "Data Driven Decision Making? Why We Ignore Data and Go With Our Guts," August 6, 2017 from URL http://datapine.com/blog/data-driven-decision-making/

Morgan, L. 2016. "Data Storytelling: What It Is, Why It Matters." February 1, 2018 from URL https://informationweek.com/big-data/big-data-analytics/data-storytelling-what-it-is-why-it-matters/a/d-id/1325544?

Newgenapps. 2018. "The 5 Benefits & Role of Cloud Computing in Digital Transformation." February 18, 2018 from URL https://newgenapps.com/blog/benefits-role-of-cloud-computing-in-digital-transformation

Newman, D. 2017. "Top 10 Trends for Digital Transformation In 2018." *Forbes*, February 14, 2018 from URL https://forbes.com/sites/daniel newman/2017/09/26/top-10-trends-for-digital-transformation-in-2018/#607e8a10293a

Panetta, K. 2016. "Gartner's Top 10 Strategic Technology Trends for 2017." *Smarter with Gartner*, October 18, 2016 from URL http://gartner.com/smarterwithgartner/gartners-top-10-technology-trends-2017

Panetta, K. 2017. "Top Trends in the Gartner Hype Cycle for Emerging Technologies." *Gartner*, February 2, 2018 from URL https://gartner.com/smarterwithgartner/top-trends-in-the-gartner-hype-cycle-for-emerging-technologies-2017/

Panetta, K. 2017. "Gartner Top 10 Strategic Technology Trends for 2018." *Smarter with Gartner*, February 14, 2018 from URL https://gartner.com/smarterwithgartner/gartner-top-10-strategic-technology-trends-for-2018/

Potter, B. 2015. "Self-Service BI vs. Data Governance." tdwi, March 17, 2018 from URL https://tdwi.org/articles/2015/03/17/self-service-bi-vs-data-governance.aspx

Power, D. "Tom Davenport Interview: Competing on Analytics." *DSSResources. com*, May 27, 2005 from URL dssresources.com/interviews/davenport/davenport05272007.html

Power, D. 2009. *Decision Support Basics*. New York, NY: Business Expert Press.

Power, D. 2018. "What Steps Can Lead to Digital Transformation?" January 13, 2018 from URL http://dssresources.com/faq/index.php?action=artikel&id=404

Power, D.J. 1982. *Acquiring Small and Medium-sized Companies: A Study of Corporate Decision Behavior*, pp. 56–60. Ph.D. Thesis, University of Wisconsin-Madison.

Power, D.J. 2001. "What Companies Have Gained a Competitive Advantage by Building a DSS?"*Ask Dan! in DSS News* 2, no. 10, May 6, 2017 from URL http://dssresources.com/faq/index.php?action=artikel&id=28

Power, D.J. 2002. *Decision Support Systems: Concepts and Resources for Managers*. Westport, CT: Greenwood/Quorum Books.

Power, D.J. 2002a. "What Is 'Real-time' Decision Support?" *DSS News* 3, no. 24, November 24.

Power, D.J. 2002b. "When Is 'Real-time' Decision Support Desirable and Needed?" *DSS News* 3, no. 25, December 8.

Power, D.J. 2003. "What Are the Characteristics of a Decision Support System?" *DSS News* 4, no. 7, March 30.

Power, D.J. 2005. "Can Computerized Decision Support Systems Impact, Eliminate, Exploit, or Reduce Cognitive Biases in Decision Making?" *DSS News* 6, no. 20, September 11, 2005 updated September 13, 2014 for Decision Support News 15, no. 19.

Power, D. 2005. "Can DSS Provide Firms with a Sustainable Competitive Advantage? If So, How?" *DSS News* 6, no. 17, July 31, updated September 30, 2012 from URL http://dssresources.com/faq/index.php?action=artikel&id=84

Power, D.J. 2006. "What was the First Computerized Decision Support System (DSS)?" *DSS News* 7, no. 27, December 31.

Power, D.J. 2007. "What Is a Modern Decision Support System?" *DSS News* 8, no. 26, December 30, 2007 from URL http://dssresources.com/newsletters/206.php (Updated March 18, 2017).

Power, D.J. 2007a. "What Are the Features of a Communications-driven DSS?" *DSS News* 8, no. 2, January 28.

Power, D.J. 2007b. "What Are the Features of a Data-driven DSS?" *DSS News* 8, no. 4, February 25.

Power, D.J. 2007c. "What Are the Features of a Document-driven DSS?" *DSS News* 8, no. 5, March 11.

Power, D.J. 2007d. "What Are the Features of a Knowledge-driven DSS?" *DSS News* 8, no. 6, March 25.

Power, D.J. 2007e. "What Are the Features of a Model-driven DSS?" *DSS News* 8, no. 7, April 8.

Power, D.J. 2008. "What Are Ethical Issues Associated with Building and Using DSS?" *DSS News* 9, no. 5, March 9, last updated April 17, 2016.

Power, D.J. 2009. "What Are Characteristics of Decision Processes?" *DSS News* 19, no. 22, January 11, 2009 from URL http://dssresources.com/faq/index.php?action=artikel&id=195

Power, D.J. 2017. "What Are Major Managerial Dilemmas of Digital Transformation?" August 21, 2017 from URL http://dssresources.com/faq/index.php?action=artikel&id=386

Power, D.J. 2017. "What Increases Success for Data-based Decision Support?" July 21, 2017 from URL http://dssresources.com/faq/index.php?action=artikel&id=388 (accessed July 21, 2017).

Power, D. J. 2017. "Couchbase research reveals a majority of organizations expect to fail in four years if digital transformation approach is unsuccessful." March 15, 2018 from URL http://dssresources.com/news/4798.php

Power, D. J. 2017. "Artificial Intelligence and analytics accelerate the pace of digital workplace transformation." March 15, 2018 from URL URL http://dssresources.com/news/4789.php.

Power, D.J., and C. Heavin. 2017. *Decision Support, Analytics, and Business Intelligence*. Business Expert Press.

Provost, F., and T. Fawcett. March 2013. "Data Science and Its Relationship to Big Data and Data-driven Decision Making." *Big Data* 1, no. 1, March 21, 2017 from URL http://online.liebertpub.com/doi/pdf/10.1089/big.2013.1508

Provost, F., and T. Fawcett. March 2013. "Data Science and Its Relationship to Big Data and Data-driven Decision Making," *Big Data* 1, no. 1, March 15, 2018 from URL http://online.liebertpub.com/doi/pdf/10.1089/big.2013.1508

Setia, P., V. Venkatesh, and S. Joglekar. 2013. "Leveraging Digital Technologies: How Information Quality Leads to Localized Capabilities and Customer Service Performance." *MIS Quarterly* 37, no. 2, pp. 565–90.

Shah, S., A. Horne, and J. Capella. 2012. "Good Data Won't Guarantee You Good Decisions." December 11, 2017 from URL https://hbr.org/2012/04/good-data-wont-guarantee-good-decision

Shea, J., J. Jones Santos, and P. Byrnes. November 2012. "Community Needs Assessment and Data-Supported Decision Making: Keys to Building Responsive and Effective Health Centers." *National Association of Community Health Centers*, February 18, 2018 from URL http://nachc.com/client/documents/2012%20Data%20Supported%20Decision%20Making.pdf

Shein, E. 2018. "Winning the War for AI Talent." February 18, 2018 from URL https://cio.com/article/3252338/artificial-intelligence/winning-the-war-for-ai-talent.html

Tchakirides, D. 2011. "Principles of Visual Design," *Slideshow*, January 21, 2018 from URL http://slideshare.net/dianetch/principles-of-visual-design-6647916#btnNext

Techopedia.com 2018. "What does Data-Driven Decision Making (DDDM) mean?" February 1, 2018 at URL https://techopedia.com/definition/32877/data-driven-decision-making-dddm

The Free Dictionary 2003. "Hard Data is Defined as Data in the Form of Numbers or Graphs, as Opposed to Qualitative Information." *McGraw-Hill Dictionary of Scientific & Technical Terms*, 6E. May 27, 2015 from URL http://encyclopedia2.thefreedictionary.com/hard+data

Trevor, J. and Varcoe, B. 2017. "How Aligned Is Your Organization?" *Harvard Business Review*, December 13, 2017 from URL https://hbr.org/2017/02/how-aligned-is-your-organization

Tufte, E. 1983; 2001 (2nd ed.). *The Visual Display of Quantitative Information*. Cheshire, CT: Graphics Press.

Tufte, E. 2001. *Envisioning Information*. Cheshire, CT: Graphics Press.

van der Meulen, R. 2018. "The Algorithm Economy Will Start a Huge Wave of Innovation." *Gartner*, February 1, 2018 from URL https://gartner.com/smarterwithgartner/the-algorithm-economy-will-start-a-huge-wave-of-innovation/

van Duin, S., and N. Bakhshi. 2018. "Part 1: Artificial Intelligence Defined—The Most Used Terminology Around AI." February 5, 2018 from URL https://www2.deloitte.com/nl/nl/pages/data-analytics/articles/part-1-artificial-intelligence-defined.html

Varian, H. 2009. "Hal Varian on How the Web Challenges Managers." August 21, 2017 from URL https://mckinsey.com/industries/high-tech/our-insights/hal-varian-on-how-the-web-challenges-managers

WestEd Data for Decisions Initiative, "Frequently Asked Questions Related to Data for Decision Making." August 21, 2017 from URL http://datafordecisions.wested.org/data-use-basics/frequently-asked-questions/

Westerman, G., D. Bonnet, and A. McAfee. 2014. "The Nine Elements of Digital Transformation." August 21, 2017 from URL http://sloanreview.mit.edu/article/the-nine-elements-of-digital-transformation/

Wikipedia. "LEO (computer)," March 15, 2018 from URL http://en.wikipedia.org/wiki/LEO_%28computer%29

Wikipedia. "Semi Automatic Ground Environment." January 5, 2018 from URL http://en.wikipedia.org/wiki/Semi_Automatic_Ground_Environment

Index

CPSIA information can be obtained
at www.ICGtesting.com
Printed in the USA
JSHW012258050320
4602JS00007B/136